THE ACADEMIC KITCHEN

SUNY Series, Frontiers in Education
Philip G. Altbach, editor

The Frontiers in Education Series draws upon a range of disciplines and approaches in the analysis of contemporary educational issues and concerns. Books in the series help to reinterpret established fields of scholarship in education by encouraging the latest synthesis and research. A special focus highlights educational policy issues from a multidisciplinary perspective. The series is published in cooperation with the School of Education, Boston College. A complete listing of the books in this series can be found at the end of this volume.

THE ACADEMIC KITCHEN

A Social History of Gender Stratification at The University of California, Berkeley

Maresi Nerad

State University of New York Press

Sections of chapter one previously appeared as "The Situation of Women at Berkeley between 1870–1915," by Maresi Nerad, in *Feminist Issues* 7:1, 1987. Copyright ©1987 by Transaction Publishers; all right reserved. Reprinted by permission of Transaction Publishers.

Production by Ruth Fisher
Marketing by Anne M. Valentine

Published by
State University of New York Press, Albany

For information, address the State University of New York Press, State University Plaza, Albany, NY 12246

Library of Congress Cataloging-in-Publication Data

Nerad, Maresi.
    The academic kitchen : a social history of gender stratification at the University of California, Berkeley/Maresi Nerad.
        p.   cm.—(SUNY series, frontiers in education).
    Includes bibliographical references and index.
    ISBN 0-7914-3969-0 (hc : acid free). —ISBN 0-7914-3970-4 (pb : acid free)
    1. University of California, Berkeley. Dept. of Home Economics—History. 2. Home Economics—Study and teaching (Higher)—California—History. 3. Women college teachers—California—History. 4. Women—Education (Higher)—California—History. 5. Feminism and education—California—History. I. Title. II. Series.
TX285.U52N47 1999   98-11597
640'.71'1794—dc21   CIP

10 9 8 7 6 5 4 3 2 1

To
my mother and friend,
Dr. Dorothea Nerad

CONTENTS

List of Illustrations

LIST OF TABLES

Acknowledgments

At the end of a long process that began with writing a dissertation, progressed to revising it into an integrated story of institutional and biographical history, and concluded with critically rethinking the manuscript after years of working in the belly of the central administration of the University of California, Berkeley, it is a pleasure to acknowledge and thank the many colleagues and friends who contributed to this book.

I first became interested in Berkeley's home economics department when I attended Frederick Rudolph's inspiring seminar on the history of higher education.

At the first stage of my research, Guy Benveniste sharpened my understanding of the functioning of bureaucracies in times of uncertainty, crisis, and expansion. Geraldine Clifford's own research and knowledge of the history of women in higher education provided leads and helped explain events at Berkeley. Her thoughtful reading strengthened the early work. Arlie Hochschild encouraged me to place women, not organizations, at the center of this research. Martin Trow's work on prestige and status in higher education provided a base upon which to build.

This research was supported by the University of California Bancroft Library Study Award, the Phi Lambda Theta Dissertation Scholarship Award, and the Education Improvement Grant of the Graduate Assembly. After receiving my Ph.D. and starting work in the Graduate Division as its central researcher, Joseph Cerny, dean of the Graduate Division, allowed me time off from work and the use of the Graduate Division's resources to revise and complete this manuscript.

William Roberts, the university archivist, helped me find many important materials and guided me in using them. He always made me feel welcome in my quest for information, as did the entire staff of the Bancroft Library. I also wish to thank Bill, as university archivist, for granting permission to reproduce some of the photographs that illustrate this book. Thanks also to Transaction Press for granting permission to quote from my previous article in *Feminist Issues*. It is a pleasure to acknowledge and to thank the Regional Oral History Office, especially its directors, Willa Baum and Ann Lage, for the tremendous work they have done in collecting local oral histories and for granting permission to quote from these interviews.

This story could not have been pieced together without the willingness of several faculty members of the former Department of Home Economics, later the Department of Nutritional Science, as well as members of previous university administrations to share their memories, files, and pictures with me: the late George Briggs, Doris Calloway, the late Catherine Landreth, Angela Little, Clark Kerr, and Mary Ann Williams. Lilian Morgan, Agnes Fay Morgan's daughter-in-law, was supportive of this research and helped search for Morgan's papers.

Marian Gade and Janet Ruyle provided important input along the way. Marian, who is uniquely familiar with the University of California history and an expert in higher education, gave generously of her time, and Janet made the Center for Studies in Higher Education's resources available to me.

This book owes much to Jeanette Hopkins, who took a personal interest in the story and masterfully helped to develop it. Debra Sands Miller ploughed through difficult-to-read handwriting and helped create a new readable manuscript. Nancy Chapman and especially Jean Six looked out for inconsistencies and Jean helped the manuscript through its final steps. John Turner reproduced the photographs and Theresa Melango designed the book's cover.

The intellectual contributions of Margaret Rossiter and John Thelin go beyond timely referee reports. Margaret's own two volumes of the history of American women scientists provided guidance and assurance along the way that my research was on track. The citations and scribbled notes I received from her from time to time from her journeys through the archives and her occasional visits to Berkeley helped bring me back to our shared interest in history, which I greatly needed, as my present life is deeply imbedded in current research on graduate education. John Thelin has become a mentor, cherished colleague, and dear friend during the process of completing this book. His unfailing encouragement and enthusiasm for this research sustained me during my pursuit.

My most sincere thanks goes to Philip Altbach. His persistence and cajoling brought this book to see the light of day.

Friends played a very special role during the process of this work. They read and commented on early versions and listened to presentations on the subject: "Dissertation Liberation Front" with Sigrid Brauner, Pat Hayashi, Rita Maran, and Walter Wang; the "Women and Work Group"; Edith Hoshino; and in later stages Renate Sadrozinski and Susanne von Paczensky. Gloria Bowles and Renate Klein sparked many hot debates about organizational strategies of women's studies programs and stimulated my thinking along feminist lines. Not only was Anne Machung a friend with whom I could share all my highs and lows about this work and get constructive advice, but also she was the most engaged critic of my work. I could always count on the late Sigrid Brauner, Regula Langeman, Evelyn Schaefer, Susan Belkin, Ayse Yonder, and Susan Chandler for moral support.

My mother, Dorothea Nerad, and my sister, Sigrid Berndt, always supported me, although they were geographically far away.

Throughout the long process Kannan Krishnan stood by my side with imaginative, steadfast support and plenty of humor. I thank him. Will I ever be able to make up for the many changed travel plans?

INTRODUCTION

This book tells the story of the rise and fall of an all-women's department at a major public university, the University of California, Berkeley. It is also the story of Agnes Fay Morgan, one of the early women to earn a Ph.D. in science. The unique focus of this book on the connection between gender and status in an academic department, and the role of gender and status during the life of a woman scientist who was instrumental in developing that department, presents a challenge to organizational theorists, higher educational specialists, and particularly historians of higher education to rethink the traditional assessment of academic departments and the writing of biography.[1]

Including gender in the analysis exposes the process by which departments dominated by women—education, library science, nursing, social welfare, women's physical education, and home economics—began in the 1900s as separate, unequal institutions, low in status and prestige, as a place to put the rising number of women students and women faculty. These departments struggled along with little support, only to be terminated by academic administrators some fifty years later when they were no longer useful, or, if they persevered, they did so without economic rewards, prestige, or power. In times of budgetary crises, these departments have been the first ones targeted for closure.

By including organizational theory in a biographical account, we can see the different success possible for an individual. Agnes Fay Morgan's great individual success for her published research stands in relief against the background of the neglect and derision of her equally important organizational work as home economics department chair to build and sustain a respected science department. This study disentangles hard-learned historical lessons at the University of California that may benefit newly established academic programs and, particularly, women's studies departments. In doing so this book contributes to an understanding of how universities work.

I became interested in the history of all-women's departments because of my own involvement in women's studies and my participation in the ongoing debate about the best way to advance feminist research, teaching, and learning.[2] Whether women's studies should be "mainstreamed" or become a separate department were issues of fierce debate among feminist scholars during the 1980s and into the 1990s. Proponents understood "mainstreaming" as working within a discipline to change the paradigms. Gender, they argued, should be taught as an integral part of the subject, not merely as adjacent or parallel to it. Those who argued for a separate women's studies department asserted that women's studies, if mainstreamed, would soon be swallowed up by the demands of the diverse disciplines, and any focused attention to women's issues would fade away. They reasoned that if women's studies established separate departments the young discipline gradually would develop a strong identity and the professional networks necessary for survival in an academic environment traditionally not supportive of women. As a separate and distinct department, women's studies would have its own budget, admit its own students, grant tenure to and promote its own faculty, and eventually develop its own graduate program, all features important for survival and for developing strength and status within the university community.

I felt that understanding the history of a "women's department" in a coeducational institution, specifically the formal and informal reactions of a university to such a department, could provide insight into the implications and effectiveness of the divergent strategies, or some reconciliation of them. An understanding of the process by which a new field is assimilated into the university was also necessary. I began to search for an example in university life that would fulfill both conditions. Home economics fit the bill. At universities like Chicago, Cornell, Illinois, Iowa, and Wisconsin, home economics departments had sprung up at the end of the nineteenth and the beginning of the twentieth centuries, founded by remarkable women such as Agnes Fay Morgan and dominated throughout their existence by women.

The choice of home economics as a topic of study may surprise many scholars, particularly feminist scholars. Most men scholars probably have not been exposed to home economics and know little about it. For many women the experience of home economics in junior high school, where they had to prepare eggs à la goldenrod and sew a fine seam while the boys were learning carpentry and radio and car repair, left such sour memories that everything connected with home economics seems demeaning. Although nowadays feminists are more tolerant of fields traditionally occupied by women, they are still ambivalent about home economics. To many feminists home economics implies an acceptance of the traditional, subordinated role of women in society, as well as a blindness to race and class issues, and an apolitical or nationalistic and conservative political outlook on society. As for home economists themselves, many do not consider themselves feminists and have no special interest in "women's studies." Indeed, some may equate feminism with the sexual revolution, permissiveness, and gender confusion of the sixties and seventies. But if feminist faculty can put aside their ingrained prejudice against home economics, at least in order to learn what the history of the struggle of home economics on their own campuses can tell them about women and powerlessness, they will discover the broad range of the complex dimensions of gender, enhanced by male bureaucracy, that has characterized the history of academia in the United States. If male faculty members at research universities, particularly in newly established departments, want to understand the inner process that controls rewards, prestige, and status that goes to their departments, by reading this book they will discover some of the factors that shape the university bargaining process over allocation of resources and rewards.[3]

FROM SOCIAL REFORM MOVEMENT TO ACADEMIC STUDY: HOME ECONOMICS

The University of California, Berkeley, Home Economics Department developed in the second decade of the twentieth century, but the idea of home economics education dates back to the early nineteenth century. Home economics as a field of study was first introduced in the United States before the Civil War in a curriculum of female seminars by advocates of women's higher education, such as Emma Willard, Mary Lyon, and Catherine Beecher.[4] These early advocates considered women foremost as moral guardians whose role was to save the family and, by so doing, civilize men and society. A woman's primary, even sole, social function, in their view, was "the nurturing of life," both in the home and in the community. Thus, a form of education for women was developed to prepare them for that crucial role. During the Progressive Era, even up to the end of World War I, the concept of women as the moral guardians and saviors of society had wide support.

THE HOME ECONOMICS MOVEMENT

With rapid industrialization and urbanization and a steady increase in immigration, with migration from country to city in search for jobs, and the growth of city slums, established rural values had to be adapted to new urban settings during the last quarter of the nineteenth century. The economic function of the family changed with the increase of factory-produced goods for home use across all class levels, and the character of the home changed from a place of production to a place of consumption. By the turn of the century many working-class and black women had the option of jobs in industry instead of service positions in middle and upper-class homes. An increasing number of middle-class women, whose comfort had depended on servants, had to find alternative ways to get the housekeeping done. At the same time the first generation of college-educated women were seeking jobs outside the home. In this climate, during the last quarter of the nineteenth century, the educational home economics movement burgeoned into what was first seen as a reform movement. No longer simply or primarily a means of justifying support for women's education, home economics education now became an end in itself.

Education on how to manage a household scientifically, proponents of home economics believed, could counter more than one social ill. If home economics was properly taught, men would be lured from saloons by the tasty meals cooked by cheerful and competent wives. In rural communities, women would now find country life acceptable, and thus farm conditions would improve. Middle-class women would find new meaning in their lives through scientific homemaking and social reform work, which was linked to the spread of the perfectly managed household and its promise of improved family life and ultimately an improved society. Young women headed for domestic service would be properly trained in maintaining the high standards of the American household. Home economics became a Progressive Era panacea for reforming American society. By saving the family, society itself would be saved.[5]

During the end of the nineteenth and the beginning of the twentieth centuries science and technology took on an "aura of divinity."[6] Science and technology could do no wrong, and their presence lent dignity and status to the most trivial of day-to-day household tasks. Industrialization, which had already changed the workplace, now began changing home life: the light bulb and telephone made life easier, and new knowledge about germs and calories enlightened homemakers about their vital role. Many women who crusaded for home economics training believed that if the home became a more businesslike and efficient place, if husbands were fed and children raised according to scientific principles, if purity and fresh air swept through every corner of the house, then the nation could triumph over disease, poverty, and social decay.

The principal actors in this reform movement of home economics were middle-class women, particularly, members of women's clubs, members of the Young Women's Christian Association, and members of church and philanthropic organizations. Armed by science and convinced of the power of women as moral guardians of society, they opened cooking schools in the East, set up domestic science magazines, and set up tours across the country to present lectures on the values of domestic science.[7] Home economics seemed to appeal to women of all social classes. Elite women, with no housekeeping of their own to do, could study the principles of homemaking and management and teach the skills to others. Middle-class housewives could elevate their own status and assume a professional aura and sense of personal fulfillment by running a scientifically managed home. Poor immigrant women, instructed in homemaking in the settlement houses and through charitable agencies, could integrate more rapidly into American society.

Ironically, the domestic science crusaders or "domestic feminists," as Karen Blair has called them, looked upon the reform movement as transforming their own ignorant, backward sisters.[8] They blamed the unschooled, traditional American housewife, the uneducated working-class women, and the immigrant women for the poverty in American homes, for disease, for the abuse of alcohol, and for the high infant mortality rates. In contrast, suffragist leaders were concerned that poverty, infant mortality, and diseases were a consequence of political and economic conditions and of the patriarchal social structure, not of women's own ignorance. They did not support the idea of teaching special courses for women. They demanded exactly the same education for women as was available to men. The women's colleges of the East—Vassar, Radcliffe, Barnard, Wellesley, Smith, and Mount Holyoke—operated upon this principle, as evidenced by Martha Carey Thomas, president of Bryn Mawr from 1894 to 1922, who enforced the same academic rigor for her female students as was demanded from male students at Harvard, Yale, or other elite men's colleges.[9] Competing beliefs of the suffragists and the domestic science crusaders regarding the content of women's education were also present in many of the newly emerging universities.

THE ACADEMIC STUDY OF HOME ECONOMICS

Home economics as a field of academic study initially was shaped by a series of ten annual fall conferences held at Lake Placid, Morningside, New York, from 1899 to 1908. Ellen Richards, then head of the Women's Laboratory for the instruction of women in science at the Massachusetts Institute of Technology, initiated the first meeting with the support of Melvil Dewey, director of the State Library in the State of New York and an influential figure in the movement for a "profession" of library work. Eight women representing various women's interest groups from New York and

Boston took part in the formative conferences: educators from state normal schools: Alice P. Norton, later at the University of Chicago; Louise A. Nicholass, of the State Normal School at Framingham; Anna Barrows, later of Teachers College of Columbia University; Maria Daniell, a pioneer in institutional management; Maria Parloa, a teacher in the famous Boston Cooking School; Emily Huntington, the first teacher of the famed Kitchen Garden classes in New York City; Mrs. W. G. Shailer, president of the New York Household Economics Association (part of the Federation of Women's Clubs); and Mrs. W. Kellen, an activist in the promotion of a Boston public school lunch program. The goal that evolved from the meeting was to make home economics respectable as an academic discipline and to lay the groundwork for home economics as a profession. The conference ended by recommending that state legislatures give to home economics the "same practical encouragement which they now give to agriculture and the mechanic arts in state schools and colleges."[10]

The participants in the Lake Placid conferences, whose numbers grew from eleven in 1899 to 202 in 1908, systematically developed course syllabi for elementary schools, colleges, and university extension programs. They debated degree requirements for home economics as an academic program and tried to standardize the nomenclature. The most commonly used definition of home economics dates from 1902, the year of the fourth Lake Placid conference.

Home economics in its most comprehensive sense is the study of laws, conditions, principles and ideals which are concerned on the one hand with man's immediate physical environment and on the other hand with his nature as a social being, and is the study specifically of the relation between those two factors. In a narrow sense the term is given to the study of the empirical sciences with special reference to the practical problems of housework, cooking, etc.[11]

The "narrower sense" is the term most people today associate with home economics. The broader definition, as set forth at the conference, resonates with present-day discussions in ecological circles and environmental studies groups. At the seventh and eighth Lake Placid conferences, Ellen Richards stressed the broad definition by arguing for a "science of controllable environment" or a science that would study the necessary modification of the environment in order to ensure "sane well balanced citizens."[12] By this she meant that home economics should concern itself with the material conditions of living. During the first decades of the twentieth century academic women teaching at universities such as M.I.T., Chicago, Columbia, Cornell, and Berkeley would proceed along the lines of the broader, not the narrower, definition. For male administrators it was another story; to them the narrow definition was the only one.

The field of home economics was understood to have four subdivisions: food, clothing, shelter, and household and institutional management, each representing the broad as well as the narrow definition. In each category emphasis was to be placed on "the relation of chemistry, physics, mathematics, biology, economics, aesthetics, and engineering to the various subdivisions." This broad and diffuse understanding of the field drew extremely diverse followers and tended to make it difficult for the field to develop a clear academic and professional identity. "Sewing" and "cooking" or "manual training," or "handwork" was proposed for girls in public elementary schools, "domestic science" for public secondary schools, and "home economics" for students in colleges and universities. It represented a hierarchy and a class distinction with a craft orientation at the lowest level and a scientific and professional orientation at the highest level.

At the final Lake Placid conference, in 1909, representatives from thirty-seven states, Canada, and England attended, their efforts culminating in the formation of a professional organization, the American Home Economics Association (AHEA), and the establishment of a professional journal, *The Journal of Home Economics*. The new association started with a membership of seven hundred. Ellen Swallow Richards was its first president.[13]

AHEA immediately set out to spread the idea of home economics instruction in schools, colleges, and universities, and with prompt success. Members of the AHEA participated in many conferences and on special committees of educational associations. They worked together with the Association of Agricultural Colleges and Experiment Stations to specify syllabi of home economics training for all levels of education. The annual meetings were purposely held at the same places and at the same time as the meetings of related professional or academic associations. So, for example, in 1909, the AHEA met in Boston, the site of the meeting of the annual American Association for the Advancement of Science (AAAS). In 1910, their meeting was in St. Louis, along with meetings of the American Sociological Society and the American Economics Association; economists and sociologists attending the latter meetings also presented their ideas about home economics to AHEA sessions, while home economists lectured to the sociology and economics group. Thus, the idea of home economics as an academic field of study was disseminated and supported widely within academic and professional circles.

In 1912, under the leadership of Julia Lathrop, a Vassar graduate, the federal government established the United States Children's Bureau, which reinforced a public focus on "Home and Women." In 1915, two members of the AHEA joined the staff of the U.S. Bureau of Education as specialists in home economics,[14] and information on educational issues in home economics was published broadly through the Bureau. "By 1916," writes Isabel Bevier, "the foundations of home economics were fairly well settled in the curricula of many types of schools."[15]

Firm institutionalization of the field of home economics in schools and land-grant colleges and universities came with the passage of the Smith-Lever Act of 1914 and the Smith-Hughes Act of 1917. The Smith-Lever Act provided ten thousand dollars each year for each state to distribute to public agricultural colleges for agricultural extension work; it was intended to "aid in diffusing among the people of the U.S. useful and practical information on subjects relating to agriculture and home economics and to encourage the application of the same."[16] Consequently, many, but not all, land grant colleges began to offer home economics courses through their extension programs.

The Smith-Hughes Act, also known as the Vocational Education Act, made monies available to the states on a matching fund basis for teacher training and teacher salaries in three designated areas: agriculture, trade education, and home economics.[17] The Smith-Hughes Act directly affected home economics teacher training in land-grant institutions. Previously incidental to other objectives of home economics instruction, teacher training now became the primary objective in many institutions. Most of the schools that sought federal aid to help pay teachers' salaries began to require that all girls in public schools study home economics. This, in turn, created a demand for teachers in the lower grades and for teacher trainers, directors, and supervisors of those programs at the college level. The Smith-Hughes Act paid the salaries of teachers in agriculture, trades and industry, and home economics below college level and, in addition, subsidized teacher training courses at the college level by paying the salaries of teachers, directors, and supervisors of these courses, as well as the salaries of clerical help.

Thus, home economics in institutions of higher education became tied to teacher training. The concept of home economics was now understood as a vocation in the public mind, which was for the future development of the field both a blessing and a curse. A blessing, because it allowed many women to find paid employment as home economists and home economics teachers; a curse, because it legitimized further the concept of sex-differentiated and unequal educational programs in high schools, colleges, and universities.

Male educators, and especially university presidents of the Progressive Era, welcomed the new subject of domestic science as a proper field for women students—one that would train them for their destined vocation of wife and mother. When, at the beginning of the century, there was a sudden influx of women students into the university, top-level administrators, male, began to fear that these new women students would drive men out of the College of Letters and Liberal Arts. A department of home economics, they became convinced, would pursue a separate—and appropriate—dominion for women faculty and students. At the same time, many agricultural constituencies were lobbying to establish home economics programs to train women homemakers in rural communities to contribute to a healthier, better farm life and, as a consequence, stem the growing flight from rural areas to urban areas.

Fledgling research universities, such as Chicago, Cornell, Michigan, Illinois, and Berkeley, which did establish home economics programs in these years in order to broaden women's employment opportunities and to respond to the increase in female enrollment, nonetheless sought to distance themselves from any campus program that might take on the character of vocational training and thus weaken their own academic and research reputations. However, supporters of home economics from outside the university, often motivated by conflicting interests, confronted the home economics departments at coeducational research universities, seeking to reinforce the practical aspects of home economics. Home economics departments, specifically at research universities, were caught in a dilemma: they had to adhere to academic values of basic research in order to survive, but if they did, they risked alienating their home economics supporters and constituencies in the professional field who expected practical advice and training from the university.

THE BERKELEY SAGA

Between 1905 and 1916 home economics was introduced at Berkeley primarily as an administrative strategy to isolate the many women students now registering in the College of Letters and Science and to minimize their competition with men. This was the administration's intent even if the president's articulated purposes made other more practical claims. At the same time, the introduction of home economics provided a way to prepare women for, what was seen by society in general, and Berkeley's male administration in particular, as their ultimate vocation, that of marriage and motherhood.

Women themselves, inside and outside the university at Berkeley, promoted home economics in an entirely different spirit. They envisioned home economics as potentially broadening women's employment opportunities, pressing the university to set up a school of home economics, with five subdivisions addressing the problems of food, clothing, housing, household administration, and household education. Their aims, in various ways, were distorted by the president of the university; they were never fully realized, because of lack of administrative support, money, visibility, status, and power. This book demonstrates how this happened.

Home economics at the University of California, Berkeley, began as a liberal arts undergraduate program in a department of home economics within the College of Letters and Science, with two divisions: household arts and household science. The new program had little autonomy and was low in status and prestige, until, in 1918, an extraordinary woman, Agnes Fay Morgan, with a doctorate in organic chemistry from the University of Chicago, became chair of the household science division of the department. She reorganized the new program into an independent Department of Household Science, housed first within the College of Letters and Sciences, and, then, after 1930, within the College of Agriculture, where the department was renamed Home Economics.

Chairing the department for thirty-six years, Morgan gave the department a clear identity. She redesigned the undergraduate liberal arts curriculum, focusing on a rigorous basic orientation to science and research. The resulting program enabled graduating home economics students to continue in graduate work and to earn a Ph.D. through a new Berkeley interdepartmental graduate group in nutrition. Through participation in many professional organizations, Morgan acquired visibility on and off campus, supporting her endeavors to attract funds and cooperation for various research projects. Through her boundless energy and her administrative ability to separate the essential from the trivial, she ingeniously found ways to offset an extremely limited research budget, insufficient laboratory equipment, and inadequate space. Because her efforts and those of her colleagues Ruth Okey and Catherine Landreth led to important research findings, the department came to rank high in reputation among home economics programs in American universities. Between 1918 and 1962, thirty-one doctorates and 165 master's degrees were awarded to Berkeley home economics students. Yet on the Berkeley campus, home economics never gained respect. The department was compelled to struggle continually to legitimize and defend its academic standards and the status of its faculty and students.

The effectiveness of the strategies Dr. Morgan used to upgrade the departmental status—strategies that usually sufficed in all-male departments—was reduced, even nullified, because of gender, and because home economics was an applied field engaged in the practical pursuits of helping society.[18] The interplay of strategies applied by the university administration toward departments and vice versa is the key focus of this book.

Women were seen, by definition and physiology, as subordinate to men and of lesser worth. Power for women seemed to male administrators and faculty a contradiction in terms. The Berkeley case demonstrates how status, power, and prestige go hand-in-hand with gender. Once the home economics department at Berkeley was established specifically to train women to become better wives and mothers, the university president and the male faculty considered it a strictly vocational field. As such, it never could measure up to high academic standards and was deemed undeserving of equal funding, equipment, salaries, power, and status.

Simply because they were women, Agnes Fay Morgan and her colleague Ruth Okey, as well as many other women similarly well trained in chemistry in the early part of the twentieth century, never found employment in departments of chemistry or biochemistry and had no choice but to work in home economics departments. In consequence, they had no access to research money from within and without the university other than funds specifically designated for problems concerning food, family, and children. Their research, performed professionally despite overwhelming obstacles, was never valued by professional associations such as the American Institute of Nutrition or by many research universities, despite their often significant scientific contributions.

The public equated home economics with teacher training alone, and, reflecting this bias, faculty members from neighboring disciplines, such as biochemistry and anatomy, assumed home economics doctoral students were less analytically skilled and less original and rigorous in their research. As a result these well-trained students were scrutinized excessively and often required to take additional course work not required of male doctoral degree candidates before they were permitted to advance to candidacy.

The evidence in this story will show that because home economics at Berkeley was established as a department specifically for women, headed by a woman, and, therefore, of academically low prestige, during the tenure of its founder, Agnes Fay Morgan, it was never allowed to change its name to *human nutrition*, as she repeatedly proposed. The designation *human nutrition* was seen as encroaching upon the male domains of animal nutrition, biochemistry, and food technology. Only after Morgan retired, succeeded by a man, George Briggs, and applied home economics was transferred to the Davis campus, did the campus administration allow the department to change its name to *Nutritional Science*. Given the research produced by the department and the successful employment of its students, criteria necessary for its academic acceptance, it probably would have ranked fairly high in status on the Berkeley campus from its first years had home economics not been designated women's work and had the department not been staffed and led by women only. The original department was never able to raise its status to a position comparable to male-led applied fields. Agnes Fay Morgan succeeded in gaining status and recognition on campus, but really, it did not reach beyond herself.

Even the scientific contributions of the pioneering Agnes Fay Morgan were silenced. At the retirement celebration of her successor, in a history of nutrition at Berkeley narrated by Norman Kretschmer, then chair of the new Department of Nutritional Science,[19] the origins at Berkeley were chronicled as beginning in 1962. All the work of the Department of Home Economics and all of the thirty-nine years of Dr. Morgan's achievements in nutrition research were ignored by the speaker.[20]

Dr. Morgan's accomplishments were silenced quite effectively in other ways as well. After her death only half of her departmental files were retained by the university archives, and, even so, none of this material was indexed as was the material of other outstanding campus faculty. The travel logs from her professional trips to Europe in 1931 and 1936, when she visited all the major nutrition research laboratories in Europe, considered irrelevant by a former university archivist, were not even acquired for the archives.[21] The silencing of women's achievements was thus reinforced and perpetuated.

The case of home economics at Berkeley clearly and forcefully demonstrates the significance of gender in ranking academic departments. The inferior status of the women's departments reflects the inferior status of women in society at large. As long as women's work is devalued and women are forced to work within narrow boundaries, departments led and taught primarily by women will continue to rank low in status.

With the first course offerings in home economics at Berkeley at the turn of the century, gender stratification of academic programs was officially introduced at the University of California. But universities, including Berkeley, are still stratified along gender lines. In 1995, only 20 percent of tenured faculty were women and 80 percent men; 80 percent of the clerical work force were women and 20 percent men. The majority of the women faculty are still in traditionally female fields: the humanities (broadly defined), education, library sciences, and nutrition, while men dominate virtually every other discipline. In 1976, after four years of proposal writing and various course offerings on "women," a women's studies program was established at Berkeley.[22] Women doctoral students together with young women faculty were the driving force behind the new program. In 1986, the first women's studies faculty position was created. In all, it took fifteen years to turn the program into a department with its own budget, faculty, and students. This was accomplished finally in in 1991. Berkeley was not alone in this development. Other universities established similar separate women's studies departments. Whether the status of women in society has improved so much that women's studies programs can receive salaries, status, resources, power, and prestige equivalent to other programs remains to be seen.

As women's studies departments gain momentum, home economics departments, where they still exist, are experiencing a deep identity crisis. A dialogue between home economists and women's studies scholars may well prove invaluable. Such a dialogue may help home economics departments find a place in the twenty-first century[23] or convince them to join with nutritional sciences. It may help women's studies departments to seek to avoid being marginalized and ghettoized and in times of budgetary crises from being closed down.

Lessons drawn from this book can prepare newly established departments, particularly women's studies departments and other academic programs led by women, library sciences, nursing, and education, for their struggle to exist in coeducational universities and will make them consider their strategies and options carefully.

CHAPTER 1

CREATING A DEPARTMENT OF HOME ECONOMICS AT THE UNIVERSITY OF CALIFORNIA

The introduction of home economics at Berkeley was pursued by different actors at different times for different reasons. It was first a male administrative response to the rapidly increasing numbers of women students. Later the introduction of home economics as an academic field was spearheaded by women inside and outside the university for an entirely different reason—to broaden women's domain in higher education and to increase employment opportunities for university-trained women.

In 1905 course offerings in home economics appeared for the first time in the summer session bulletin of the University of California. The catalog announced two courses in "Domestic Science and Cookery," one course in the "Care of the Home: The fundamental principles of household economy; selection of building site, plans, sanitation, furnishing, and care of the house," and one course in "Chafing Dish Cookery: The preparation of salads, desserts, etc." (like the others, offered for two credits).[1]

Benjamin Ide Wheeler, president of the University of California from 1899 through 1919, "was sure that he had made a ten-strike for popularity," *The Record*, the summer session's student newspaper said when he introduced the courses in the summer curriculum since four-fifths of the summer students were women. Much to his surprise and dismay the courses attracted very few students. Two courses had to be canceled when not enough students signed up. The *Record* reporter explained: "It has become painfully certain that these courses are a failure. Despite the fact that this phase of the University curriculum was President Wheeler's pet project, not enough women now attending the session have registered in these courses to make it worthwhile to continue the work....The failure of the subject to attract the students, the majority of whom are women," the *Record* said pointedly, "seems indicative [of the fact] that housekeeping is not among the things California women want instruction on."[2]

This inauspicious start behind him, four years later President Wheeler established a faculty Committee on Home Economics. The regents of the university would formally approve a Department of Home Economics in the College of Letters and Science in 1916, eleven years after the initial course offerings. It took seven years to recruit faculty and plan curricula. Classes in the new department began in the fall of 1916 with ninety-two students, all women.

THE INVISIBLE BERKELEY WOMEN STUDENTS

The first eight women students enrolled at Berkeley in 1870, two years after the university opened its doors.[3] It was only then that the regents of the university unanimously passed the resolution to admit women.[4] These eight women were 9 percent of the student body.

The question of how University of California women could arrive so silently, when the subject of their admission to other land-grant universities had been the occasion for considerable controversy was partially answered by Mary Olney, a student at Berkeley in 1891, who said in her oral history: "No one expected women to attend the university and therefore no plans were made to keep them out."[5] In 1868, women in California were only 38 percent of the total population.[6] It was in 1874 that compulsory elementary education became required by law, and it was not until 1891 that high schools were established by state law in cities or incorporated towns of more than 1,500 people.[7] Possibly because of the limited amount of elementary and secondary schooling available to anyone, it is understandable that the legislature, which designed and approved the constitutional act creating the university, did not expect women to be qualified and interested enough to attend.

In addition, the fact that women originally were not admitted probably had much to do with the Victorian perception of women's roles. Patricia Graham described it perfectly: "Women were expected to be pious, pure, submissive, and domestic."[8] Higher education trained women mainly to be teachers, but teacher training easily could be done in normal schools. So why would they want to enter the university?

Western states, argues Geraldine Clifford, were too poor to support two high-grade educational institutions.[9] Financing a separate women's college would be too big a strain on a small state budget, and coeducation was a cheaper solution for a young state. By 1870 California had begun to feel the economic depression that had seized the rest of the country earlier. The railroad made the state accessible to unemployed workers and cheap eastern goods. For whatever reason, in 1870 women applied to the university and were admitted. In this way, the presence of women at Berkeley began as "problemless," but not quite as naturally "derived from the facts of western life" as Frederick Rudolph and others have assumed.[10]

Until 1890, Berkeley women were invisible; their existence on campus was as silent as their arrival. In fact, until 1891, women had no social or extracurricular life: no athletic programs, no facilities for social and cultural events, and no rooms for club meetings.[11] In contrast, male students of the same time were encouraged to build a campus life for themselves. Football, athletic competitions, class rituals, pranks, and fraternity parties were part of the men's social life. The Harmon Gym was built for men in 1878 and made much of this possible. By 1890 women began to resent their exclusion and, encouraged by the increasing women's enrollment, voiced their opinions in public and tried to enter campus life.

WOMEN ENROLL IN GREATER NUMBERS

The number of women at Berkeley grew more or less steadily from 1870 on. In 1875, 14 percent of the total student body were women, and by 1900 46 percent of the total student body were women. From then on the ratio of women to men remained fairly steady until 1915 (see table 1.1).[12] In real numbers the student body grew from 42 women in 1875 to 62 in 1880, to 105 in 1890, to 1,027 in 1900, and 2,739 in 1915. In 1900 the University of California had more women students than any other coeducational institution in the country.[13]

Between 1900 and 1914 the majority of women undergraduates at Berkeley (around 70 percent) enrolled in the College of Social Sciences. Next in preference were the College of Letters (classical courses) and the College of Natural Sciences. In 1915, when the colleges of letters, social sciences, and natural sciences were combined into one College of Letters and Science, 98 percent of all undergraduate women were enrolled in this college. Only 2 percent were scattered among the other eight colleges—agriculture, chemistry, commerce, civil engineering, mechanics, mining, medicine, and jurisprudence (see tables 1.2, 1.3, and 1.4), fields where few jobs were open to women. The numbers of men in the College of Letters and Science increased, but the proportion of all male undergraduates in the College fell, 48 percent in 1915 and 1916, as increasing numbers of men enrolled in the professional colleges. The College of Letters and Science began to resemble a women's college. Women were completing their undergraduate and graduate degrees as successfully as were men (tables 1.5 and 1.6 and figure 1).

GRADUATE WOMEN AT BERKELEY

The proportion of women in the graduate student population was higher after 1900 than of women in the undergraduate population (see tables 1.7 and 1.8). In 1905 graduate women actually outnumbered graduate men 196 to 155 (56 percent), but this was unique in Berkeley's history, and by 1910 the figure was at 49 percent. The growth can be explained in part by labor market factors: school teaching was the major occupational destination of women graduates, and a fifth university year was required in order to teach in

California's high schools. (A bachelor's degree required four years of course work.)

The first Ph.D. conferred on a woman at Berkeley was earned by Millicent Shinn, in education in 1898,[14] the second in 1900 by Jessica Peixotto in political science. In 1909 Peixotto became the chair of the Domestic Science Committee and in 1918 the first woman to reach the status of full professor at Berkeley. Fifteen women had earned Ph.D.s by 1915, with a few exceptions in the natural sciences: five in zoology, three in astronomy, one each in mathematics, physiology, and botany. Only one woman earned a doctorate in English—the traditional choice of women—and one in philosophy.

BENJAMIN IDE WHEELER OF BERKELEY: "A WOMANLY EDUCATION TO BE MORE SERVICEABLE WIVES AND MOTHERS"

The growing number of women, concentrated at the undergraduate level in a few fields, alarmed Benjamin Ide Wheeler, then

Figure 1. Berkeley students sign up for fall classes, 1920 (University of California Archives)

Table 1.1: Enrollment by Sex at the University of California, Berkeley, between 1870 and 1915

Year	Men	Women	Total	% Women
1870–71	85	8	93	9%
1875–76	268	42	310	14%
1880–81	184	62	246	25%
1885–86	201	42	243	17%
1890–91	352	105	457	23%
1895–96	811	525	1,336	39%
1900–01	1,202	1,027	2,229	46%
1905–06	1,647	1,192	2,839	42%
1910–11	2,343	1,403	3,746	37%
1915–16	3,507	2,739	6,246	44%

Source: Verne Stadtman, ed., *The Centennial Record of the University of California*, (1967): 214–24.

Table 1.2: Undergraduate Enrollment by Sex at the University of California, Berkeley, between 1870 and 1915

Year	Undergraduate Men	Women	Total	% Women
1870–71	82	8	90	9%
1875–76	263	42	305	14%
1880–81	184	62	246	25%
1885–86	192	40	232	17%
1890–91	332	100	432	23%
1895–96	738	480	1,218	39%
1900–01	1,107	951	2,058	46%
1905–06	1,504	1,015	2,519	40%
1910–11	2,096	1,176	3,272	36%
1915–16	3,001	2,285	5,286	43%

Source: Verne Stadtman, ed., *The Centennial Record of the University of California*, (1967): 214–24

Table 1.3: Undergraduates by College and Sex at the University of California, Berkeley, between 1900 and 1915

College or School	1900–1901*		1905–1906**		1910–1911**		1914–1915		1915–1916***	
	Men	Women	Men	Women	Men	Women	Men	Women	Men	Women
Letters	109	172	65	129	59	113	79	114	0	0
Social Sciences	276	650	290	764	365	786	575	1,296	1,455	2,232
Natural Sciences	80	98	88	103	349	260	746	591	0	0
Commerce	38	3	149	5	258	5	298	13	310	30
Agriculture	36	6	115	8	270	10	532	21	537	28
Mechanics	158	1	267	0	294	0	361	0	345	0
Mining	216	0	271	0	209	0	102	0	93	0
Civil Eng.	74	0	211	0	236	0	234	0	196	0
Chemistry	120	21	48	6	55	2	69	5	102	4
Medicine	0	0	0	0	27	3	42	7	31	5
Jurisprudence	0	0	0	0	0	0	0	0	67	2
At Large	0	0	0	0	0	0	3	7	0	0
Total	1,107	951	1,504	1,015	2,122	1,179	3,041	2,054	3,136	2,301
(Total as given in report)	1,107	951	1,504	1,015	2,122	1,179	3,041	2,054	3,001	2,285

Source: "Statistical Addenda," *Annual / Biennial Reports of the President*

    *1900–1902, p. 227
    **1914–1915, p. 411
    ***1918–1919, p. 316

Table 1.4: Undergraduates by College and Sex at the University of California, Berkeley, between 1895 and 1915

College or School	1900–1901		1905–1906		1910–1911		1914–1915	
	Men	Women	Men	Women	Men	Women	Men	Women
Letters	9.9%	18.2%	4.3%	12.7%	2.8%	9.5%	2.5%	5.7%
Social Sciences	24.9%	68.3%	19.3%	75.3%	17.2%	66.7%	18.9%	63.1%
Natural Sciences	7.2%	10.3%	5.9%	10.1%	16.4%	22.1%	24.5%	28.8%
Commerce	3.4%	0.3%	9.9%	0.5%	12.2%	0.4%	9.8%	0.6%
Agriculture	3.3%	0.6%	7.6%	0.8%	12.7%	0.8%	17.5%	1.0%
Mechanics	14.3%	0.1%	17.8%	0.0%	13.9%	0.0%	11.9%	0.0%
Mining	19.5%	0.0%	18.0%	0.0%	9.8%	0.0%	3.4%	0.0%
Civil Eng.	6.7%	0.0%	14.0%	0.0%	11.1%	0.0%	7.7%	0.0%
Chemistry	10.8%	2.2%	3.2%	0.6%	2.6%	0.2%	2.3%	0.2%
Medicine					1.3%	0.3%	1.5%	0.3%
Jurisprudence	0.0%	0.0%	0.0%	0.0%	0.0%	0.0%	0.0%	0.3%
At Large	0.1%	0.0%	0.0%	0.0%	0.0%	0.0%	0.0%	0.0%
Total (Total as given in report)	100.0%	100.0%	100.0%	100.0%	100.0%	100.0%	100.0%	100.0%

Source: "Statistical Addenda," *Annual/Biennial Reports of the President, 1900–1902, 1914–1915*

president of the university. In his first biennial report to the governor in 1900, Wheeler devoted nearly an entire page to the "rising proportion of women students."[15] In 1902 he noted that the university had more women students than any other coeducational institution in the nation.[16] With 46 percent of its student population female in 1900, Berkeley was more than 10 percent above the national average for female enrollment.[17] Between 1905 and 1916 the number of women students had more than doubled, from 1,192 to 2,944.

In 1899,[18] Stanford had established a quota of 500 women students; in that year Berkeley was already enrolling around 1,000 women. Wheeler, worried that the number would rise as women turned down by Stanford sought admission to Berkeley, stated in his biennial report for 1910 through 1912, "It must be expected that the restriction now coming to be exercised at Stanford University in the number of women students will naturally be felt in an increasing number with us."[19]

Table 1.5: Bachelor's Degrees by Sex at the University of California, Berkeley, between 1870 and 1914

Bachelor's Degrees		Women		Men		Total
A.B.	(1870–1914)	547	53%	493	47%	1,040
B.L.	(1894–1914)	1,794	70%	784	30%	2,578
Ph.B.	(1894–1906)	120	43%	156	57%	276
B.S.	(1894–1914)	468	51%	446	49%	914
Ph.B.	(1873–1893)	58	17%	288	83%	346
Total		2,987	58%	2,167	42%	5,154

A.B. in the College of Letters (classical course);
B.L. in the College of Social Sciences;
Ph.B. (1894–1906) in the College of Social Sciences;
B.S. in the College of Natural Sciences;
Ph.B. (1873–1893) in all other Colleges (Agriculture, Chemistry, Commerce, Civil Engineering, Mechanics, Engineering, Mining).

Source: *Summary of Degrees and Certificates Awarded by the University of California 1864–1933/34*, compiled by the registrar, 1934.

Table 1.6: Bachelor's Degrees by Sex at the University of California, Berkeley between 1900 and 1915

Bachelor's Degrees	1900–1901			1905–1906			1910–1911			1914–1915			1915–1916		
	Men	Women	%	Men	Women	%	Men	Women	%	Men	Women	%	Men	Women	%
A.B.	19	19	50.0%	14	37	72.5%	8	31	79.5%	11	24	68.6%	201	310	60.7%
B.L.	37	50	57.5%	36	108	75.0%	49	108	68.8%	111	171	60.6%	0	0	0
Ph.B.	4	3	42.9%	0	0	0	0	0	0	0	0	0	0	0	0
B.S.	76	13	14.6%	109	25	18.7%	181	25	12.1%	259	218	45.7%	218	20	8.4%
Total	136	85	38.5%	159	170	51.7%	238	164	40.8%	381	419	52.4%	419	330	44.1%

A.B.   equals today's B.A. Bachelor of Arts;

Ph.B.   Bachelor of Philosophy in Modern Languages, Social Sciences, and Natural Sciences, existed between 1873 and 1907;

B.L.   Bachelor of Letters granted in the College of Social Sciences, existed between 1883–1915;

B.S.   Bachelor of Science, granted in the College of Natural Sciences and all other professional Colleges (Commerce, Agriculture, Mechanics, Mining, Civil Engineering, and Chemistry).

Source: "Statistical Addenda," *Annual Reports of the President, 1900–1916.*

Table 1.7: Graduate Enrollment by Sex at the University of California, Berkeley, between 1870 and 1915

Year	Men	Graduate Women	Total	Women %
1870–71	3	—	3	—
1875–76	5	—	5	—
1880–81	—	—	—	—
1885–86	9	2	11	18%
1890–91	20	5	25	20%
1895–96	73	45	118	38%
1900–01	100	83	183	45%
1905–06	155	196	351	56%
1910–11	258	243	501	49%
1915–16	535	479	1,014	47%

Source: Verne Stadtman, ed., *The Centennial Record of the University of California*, (1967): 214–24

Table 1.8: Master's Degrees by Sex at the University of California, Berkeley, between 1891 and 1915

Master's Degrees*	Women		Men		Total
M.A.	190	53.7%	164	46.3%	354
M.L.(L.)	2	100.0%	0	0.0%	2
M.L. (SocSc)	165	65.7%	86	34.3%	251
M.S.	90	25.9%	257	74.1%	347
Total	447	46.9%	507	53.1%	954

M.L. (L.) in the College of Letters—literary course
M.L. (SocSc) in the College of Social Sciences
*Master's of Engineering and graduates in Education are not included.

Source: *Summary of Degrees and Certificates Awarded by the University of California*, 1864–1933/34, compiled by the registrar, 1934.

Wheeler's ideas about women's education were similar to those of many prominent progressive educators of his time, including Charles Eliot, president of Harvard; Stanley Hall, president of Clark University; Charles Van Hise, president of the University of Wisconsin; and Julius Sachs, professor of pedagogy at Teachers College, Columbia.[20] Although progressive educators certainly included women in their vision of a new democratic society, their vision was of a traditional woman, simply more cultured, more emotionally mature, and better educated than the average. Their key concept of education for women was education for socialization. Socialization meant roles as housewives and mothers. To Progressive Era educators motherhood was a profession (though not a profession of equal status available to men) and it never occurred to them to encourage women to achieve economic independence. After 1917, progressive educators focused on education of women within a broad liberal arts curriculum that would provide a good base for motherhood and professional consumerism.[21] In general, they favored coeducation, but a coeducation that conformed to traditional Victorian attitudes toward women—"co-" but not *together;* they believed in a separate sphere for women.

Newspaper articles quoted President Wheeler of Berkeley on the subject of women's education on various occasions, the most extended, a "heart-to-heart" talk during his first visit to the Women's Associated Student Government of Berkeley in 1904.[22] A large excerpt appeared on the front page of the *Daily Californian,* the Berkeley student newspaper, the following day.

"The public school system of California knows of no difference between men and women, and the University is part of California's public school system. But the women are not here to be like men. Womanhood is too good, too sacred, to change. Through education women should grow more true, more womanly. There is no object in trying to do what men do. . . . Her business is to be regular and orderly, not irregular and bohemian. She should not try to imitate men, to assimilate herself to a man's college. . . . Women need different organizations from the men, and they ought to have them. Their standards are different. You are not here with the ambition to be school teachers or old maids, but you are here for the preparation of marriage and motherhood. This education should tend to make you more serviceable as wives and mothers. . . . We want women for purifying, refining and upbuilding of life. Her influence should spread through the University in the interests of refinement.[23]

Wheeler's opinion about refining women through higher education was echoed by Charles E. Eliot, president of Harvard University, among others. Eliot saw the purpose of women's higher education as "developing in women the capacities and powers which will fit them to make family life more intelligent, more enjoyable, happier and more productive."[24]

President Wheeler's admonition to women not to become even school teachers carried the implication that then they might fail to marry. Not to marry carried the further implication that they would not bear children. It echoed the concept of "race suicide" much talked about by Theodore Roosevelt, a close friend of Wheeler. Roosevelt believed that if too few native-born college-bred women married and bore babies, the greater number of children of immigrants would dilute the old American stock (see figure 2).

Wheeler was evenhanded in blaming the unmarried. Unmarried men were equally criticized for evading their civic duty.

Marriage and the home are the best protectors of the state. . . . Individualism is a danger to the state. Bachelors and clubmen are the bandits, guerrillas and outcasts. I would be in favor, if it were possible to do such things by law, of a special tax on bachelors. They are the abnormalities and the abnormalities should pay the taxes.[25]

Wheeler has been portrayed by historians as one of the eminent educators of the Progressive Era for his role in elevating Berkeley from a small-town university to a leading research university.[26] He was a New Englander by birth, education, and marriage, born in 1854 to a pastor's family from Massachusetts. He earned a bachelor's and a master's degree from Brown University in 1878 and married Amey Webb, daughter of an upper-class Providence, Rhode Island family. He studied at the universities of Leipzig, Heidelberg, Jena, and Berlin, and in 1885 he received the prestigious German doctorate summa cum laude from the

Photo Courtesy
Oakland Tribune

Figure 2. Campus Events: Charter Day, 1911—U.S. President Theodore Roosevelt and UCB President Benjamin Ide Wheeler (University of California Archives)

University of Heidelberg. After a year of teaching at Harvard, he became professor of comparative philology and Greek at Cornell University, where for eleven years he headed the Greek department. During that time he taught for a year in the American School of Classical Studies in Athens. He was appointed president of the University of California in 1899. Some thought his term would "certainly be a short one,"[27] since earlier presidents had remained for only a few years, but he served as president for twenty years.

Wheeler was heralded for introducing a strong student self-government and for fostering an open "brothers-in-arms" relationship with Berkeley students, his interest and time focused on male students. He was, in effect, dean of men. He chose a private secretary each year from the Golden Bear Senior Men's Honor Society,[28] but never a woman from the women's honor society, the Prytanean.

Although partial in his attitude, Wheeler was remembered well by the early women faculty. Wheeler appointed as a dean of women Lucy Sprague, a caretaker for a close friend, George Herbert Palmer, who was a professor at Harvard.[29] Lucy Sprague was a Radcliffe graduate, young and inexperienced both in teaching and in administration. She looked up to Wheeler as a father figure "who was never surprised at my ignorance"[30] and "the easiest person to approach with any problem." It was her first full-time job after a rather sheltered and difficult life at home, an active and stimulating experience at Radcliffe, and further difficult years at the Palmer residence. She belonged to a close group of friends of Mr. and Mrs. Wheeler and, when in 1909 and 1910, Wheeler was the first official American exchange professor in Berlin (appropriately, Theodore Roosevelt Professor), she joined them.

Agnes Fay Morgan, who joined the Berkeley faculty in 1914 as assistant professor in nutrition and who served as chair of the home economics department for thirty-six years, also saw Wheeler as paternalistic, a "perfect gentleman who always stopped and graciously got off the horse and talked about the things that were going on campus,"[31] "generally a very amenable personality, but inflexible." She found him "an autocratic gentleman of the old school. . . . You could tell him your story and put up your arguments, and if he approved, all right, if not, that was the end of it."[32]

Wheeler was indeed an autocrat. He decided on all appointments of department chairs and deans and all members of the Academic Senate. He determined all salaries and all promotions and spoke for the faculty to the regents of the university. In 1916 the faculty sought unsuccessfully to introduce new bylaws into the Academic Senate to counter the president's unilateral appointments of senate committee members. Not until he retired at the end of World War I did the faculty gain more influence.[33]

Wheeler's view of women's proper role was, no doubt, shaped by his wife's own role. Amey Webb Wheeler is remembered by some as "far from being the ideal president's wife"[34] and "extremely cold and indifferent," though Lucy Sprague found her "very amusing," with "eyes that really snapped" and said she was "the most uninhibited grown-up that I have ever known." Sprague reported that she had "the highest standards of housekeeping; . . . cleanliness was, in her mind, put a little above godliness."[35] Each Sunday the couple held open house for students.[36]

Charles Van Hise, president of the University of Wisconsin from 1903 through 1918 and a close personal friend of Wheeler, before the Association of Collegiate Alumnae in 1907 aptly summarized Progressive Era educators' attitude toward home economics in the context of women's higher education and coeducation.[37] In a speech, Van Hise argued that in the early years it had posed no more problem than Asian immigrants. "The women were greatly outnumbered by the men, and the entrance of the few women made scarcely more disturbance in the work of the professors than the appearance in recent years of a considerable group of Japanese, Chinese, and Filipinos."[38]

But now, with women at Wisconsin (as at Berkeley) a larger proportion than men in the Colleges of Letters and Liberal Arts, women were "pushing the men out." It was, he concluded, a "natural tendency of sex segregation" and one he reinforced, suggesting a separate field of study for women in a department of home economics and separate sections of the same courses in those colleges of liberal arts in which "women drive men out of some subjects." A woman home economics graduate "will find the direction of her home a high intellectual pleasure rather than wearisome routine."[39] Arranging for "natural segregation," to Van Hise was a progressive approach, in contrast with the practice of private universities, such as Stanford and Wesleyan, which restricted the number of women students altogether,[40] Wesleyan after years of coeducation. Restricted admission was, however, an option only for *private* schools. To seek to reduce the number of women students at *state* universities through state legislation would have been highly controversial. In Wisconsin the regents and the state legislature both favored coeducation. However, the establishment of separate classes and "women's" subjects did not appear to breach the coeducational principle in practice.

Wheeler, in his biennial report as president of the University of California, Berkeley, hinted at this future direction of education for women's proper place.

An institution which has been named the Hearst Domestic Industries has been founded in the neighborhood of the University and provides women who desire it the opportunity of learning the handicrafts of sewing and embroidery, and of incidentally earning a fair return for their work; if the institution succeeds and represents a permanent demand as it now seems that it does, it is likely that its work will be extended in the direction of teaching cookery and related arts.[41]

Women students' need to earn a living was to Wheeler "incidental," though by teaching children in the poor area of West Berkeley to sew, cook, sweep, and clean, Berkeley women students did earn an income. According to the president's biennial report of 1900 through 1902, most Berkeley women received little financial support from home. When Wheeler introduced four domestic science classes in the summer session of 1905, he misjudged the women who actually enrolled, not women in search of household skills but, most of them, school teachers who enrolled to upgrade professional skills and knowledge.[42] The classes in "cooking" and the "care of the home" could not advance the teaching careers since, only after the passing of the Smith-Hughes Act in 1914, which provided federal money to the states to train teachers in agriculture, trade education, and home economics, were home economics classes systematically introduced in high schools across the country. Also, like the women students who worked off campus in Hearst Domestic Industries, most no doubt already knew how to cook and clean.

"ALL WE ASK IS A CHANCE": THE SECOND-CLASS STATUS OF WOMEN STUDENTS AND THE ESTABLISHMENT OF HOME ECONOMICS AT BERKELEY

The movement toward the professionalization of domestic science as "home economics" had been developing rapidly in the first decade of the twentieth century and culminated in the establishment of the American Home Economics Association in 1908.

Women were virtually shut out of science as a profession, but now the domestic role was being redefined as a science. A group of women academics, among them Ellen Swallow Richards, Marion Talbot, Isabel Bevier, and Alice Norton, picked up the challenge of applying science to "woman's domain" and dedicating themselves to making "household management, scientific cookery, and sanitary science legitimate areas of scientific inquiry." Between 1899 and 1907 Ellen Swallow Richards ran a women's laboratory at M.I.T. and organized and presided over annual Lake Placid conferences for domestic scientists. She was responsible for establishment of the American Home Economics Association and for initiation of a new professional journal, *The Journal of Home Economics*.[43] This new professional association sought to institutionalize home economics as an academic discipline. Members lectured at universities and women's clubs in an effort to rally women behind the association's objectives: to persuade universities to offer advanced degrees in home economics and to make more teaching positions available for domestic scientists.

The Association of Collegiate Alumnae (ACA), founded in 1882 to secure wider opportunities for women in and out of higher education, was ambivalent about this direction. On the one hand, a resolution of its Committee on Collegiate Administration maintained "that home economics as such has no place in a college course for women."[44] On the other hand, the ACA as a whole did endorse "sanitary science," which was the application of chemistry, biology, sociology, and law to domestic concerns, many aspects of which looked very much like home economics. The majority of the members of the ACA Committee on Collegiate Administration were from Barnard, Bryn Mawr, Vassar, and Wellesley, all eastern women's colleges. During the first two decades of the twentieth century most eastern women's colleges rejected any kind of special "women's curriculum"; their focus was on an education to enable women to compete with men on equal terms. The study of home economics not only was unequal to men's education, but because it was vocational rather than a liberal art, most of the ACA committee saw home economics as unsuitable for their curriculum. However, proponents of "sanitary science" argued that it was genuinely scientific and, besides, was intended to supplement, not replace, the liberal arts curriculum. Some of the ACA members even proposed that liberal arts for women should be taught only in graduate and professional schools. This was the approach of the San Francisco branch.

Unfazed by his abortive 1905 summer session, Wheeler established a committee four years later to design a plan for home economics on the Berkeley campus. The Domestic Science Committee (consisting of five male and two female faculty) came up with a study list in 1911, drawing on various departmental offerings. In 1914 the committee recommended a school or college of home economics to be modeled after the schools of architecture, education, and jurisprudence. The new school for women was to include teaching and research staff from the departments of architecture, chemistry, drawing, economics, engineering, hygiene, physiology, political science, and textiles. The curriculum eschewed the stereotyped training in cooking, drawing, sewing, and dressmaking, or millinery. It focused on theory and methodology, not on technical, instrumental skills. It was an effort to rethink the educated woman's role as social reform agent and as scientific and managerial professional outside the home.

In 1909 the San Francisco branch of the ACA brought Ellen Swallow Richards to Berkeley to teach during the summer session. Her two courses, "Household Management in the Twentieth Century—Relation of Cost to Efficiency" and "Euthenics," in effect had upgraded the 1905 summer session courses to courses that today would be labeled "the family and the labor market" and "public health, the family, and the state." In 1910 Dr. Sophonisba Breckinridge was appointed to teach at the Berkeley summer session courses "Public Aspects of the Household" and "The Legal and Economic Position of Women." She held a Ph.D. in political science and a J.D., both from the University of Chicago. The progressive educators' concept of home economics as instruction in cooking, sewing, and millinery now had an academic gloss and new prestige.

The California Federation of Women's Clubs, which urged Berkeley to offer home economics in its regular curriculum, continued to stress the vocation of home economics. These "domestic feminists" saw women as possessing special moral qualities and women's duty as the responsibility to apply these special abilities to the social problems of their community. Committees of the federation lobbied for pure food laws and for the introduction of domestic science into public schools with funding for teachers, equipment, and demonstrations.[45]

The federation dispatched written requests to the university for establishment of courses in domestic and household economics, citing "the evident need for such instruction and the fact that it is a fully organized and efficient branch of work in numerous institutions."[46] Along with the Berkeley women's club, the Town and Gown, it had sponsored Ellen Swallow Richards's 1909 lectures. Many of Berkeley's alumnae and women faculty belonged both to the ACA and to the women's club.[47] With easy access to women students, these club women and university alumnae exercised considerable influence. May Cheney, a Berkeley graduate of 1883 and an honorary member of the Prytaneans, the women's honor society, and the first vice president of the California ACA, was the appointment secretary of the university from 1898 to 1938. In that role she was in a position to place teachers trained on the Berkeley campus in schools around the country. With eight of ten women students in teaching, this provided a wide network of influence.

The Prytaneans honor society for women students was organized in 1901 with the help of Dr. Mary Bennet Ritter, appointed in 1898 as the first woman faculty member at Berkeley (after seven years of unpaid work for the university). She was a part-time lecturer in hygiene and a physician for women students.[48] In 1909 the Prytaneans founded the Domestic Science Club, and in 1911 they petitioned the president for university courses in home economics. When classes were offered on the "household as an economic agent" and "the child and the state" by Jessica Peixotto, lecturer in sociology and one of only three women appointed to the Berkeley faculty before 1905, the Prytaneans advertised her classes and attended them as well.

JESSICA PEIXOTTO, LUCY SPRAGUE, LUCY WARD STEBBINS: LIVING DOWN "PREJUDICES"

Women faculty members active in promoting home economics at Berkeley were Jessica Peixotto, who became assistant professor of sociology in 1907; Lucy Sprague, dean of women and assistant professor in English, beginning in 1906; and Sprague's successor, Lucy Ward Stebbins. They saw home economics as a means of advancing social reform. Sprague took her students on weekly excursions to see social conditions in San Francisco, and Peixotto arranged for graduate students to do fieldwork in the Associated Charities of San Francisco.[49] They saw home economics also as a way of broadening women's employment opportunities.

Jessica Blanche Peixotto's motto throughout her active life was "Make science serve humanity."[50] Peixotto was the oldest of five children in a prosperous American Portuguese Jewish merchant family, who moved from New York to San Francisco in 1870 when she was six. Her father became a well-known public figure, active in the city's religious and philanthropic affairs. After her secondary education at the Girls' High School of San Francisco, she hoped to enter the University of California, but her father considered university life inappropriate for a young woman with the opportunity for refinement and education in the rich cultural environment of her home. She might become an author or study music or fabric design, none of them, not incidentally, likely to win financial independence. For eleven years she gave in to her father's wishes and stayed at home with private tutoring in foreign languages and in gown design.[51] She applied her artistic skills to the designing of hats and fabrics and learned also how to manage a large and complex household, assuming the duties of one of the family housekeepers for a year. By her midtwenties she had acquired the skills that befitted an upper-class homemaker.

In 1891, when she was twenty-seven, Peixotto discovered that she could enter the university as a "special student" without a stated degree goal, and she went to Berkeley to register. Henry Rand Hatfield, professor of economics and dean of the College of Commerce, later explained that she was almost turned down because "special students" had to be eighteen and she looked ten years younger than she was.[52] For one year she took the conventional culture courses—literature, history, languages—and no science, mathematics, or economics. A male friend criticized her for wasting her time by avoiding regular student status, whereupon she enrolled in the four-year program and completed it in three years, when she entered graduate studies.

Undecided at first about a field of specialization, she opted for political science after attending classes with an inspirational teacher, Bernard Moses, and made plans to earn a doctorate. In 1896 and 1897 she received one of Phoebe Hearst's European fellowships and went to study at the Sorbonne.[53] Observing the position of women in France, she wrote to a friend and fellow doctoral student Millicent Shinn (the first woman Ph.D. at Berkeley), protesting a woman's duty to be "a divine beauty to serve her lord and master."[54] She considered the French women to be living in the Middle Ages. In 1900 she received her Ph.D., the second granted to a woman at the University of California. Her dissertation, on "A Comparative Study of the Principles of the French Revolution and the Doctrines of Modern French Socialism," was promptly published by a commercial publishing house, a rare event in academic circles.

Henry Rand Hatfield believed that Peixotto had no intention of using her doctorate, but Wheeler, who is said to have advised her to become a teacher, offered her a lectureship in "contemporary socialism" and "history of socialism in 1904," two courses with a paltry annual salary of $500. By 1906 these two courses had been broadened to embrace other varieties of social reform, such as anarchism, cooperation, and single tax. In 1907 Peixotto was named assistant professor of sociology in the economics department, with an annual salary of $1,000 (increased in 1908 to $1,500). It took eight years for her to win promotion to associate professor of social economics (with an annual salary of $2,400) and four more years to become a full professor, gaining that rank in 1918 (see figure 3). By comparison, Charles Hyde, with a B.S. from M.I.T., began at Berkeley in 1904 as an assistant professor of sanitary engineering, with an annual salary of $1,800, was promoted after three years to associate professor at $2,100, and, after another three years, to full professorship in 1910 with a salary of $2,700.

Peixotto taught social economics, a subfield of economics until World War II, offering courses not only on general social reform and economic theory, but also on "The Control of Poverty," "The Child and the State," "The Care of Dependents," "Crime as a Social Problem," and "Studies in the Standard of Living." Her course syllabi indicate that she focused on economic policies, such as tax changes, universal education, minimum wage, and public health.[55]

Figure 3. Jessica B. Peixotto, Ph.D., political science, professor of social economics 1907–1936 (photo circa 1910) (University of California Archives)

Peixotto's own life demonstrated her strong commitment to social reform and public service and to enlisting women, particularly, in "broader movements outside the university."[56] She was one of the founding members of the Berkeley Commission of Public Charities in 1910, and in 1912 she was appointed to the California State Board of Charities and Correction, serving as chair of the Committee of Children and as a chair of the Committee of Research. Under her direction the board secured enactment of legislation on the age limit under which children could receive state aid, on the licensing of midwives, and on the establishment of a separate women's reformatory. She was a pioneer in urging education and training for social workers, and her students entered social work and government, eager to cope with problems they had learned about in her classes. In 1914, together with two male colleagues, Peixotto advised Berkeley on achieving a modern, up-to-date police department by requiring two years of college training. Trainees attended Berkeley lectures, including her own. At seventy-one, she received an honorary doctorate in law from Mills College, a private women's liberal arts college, and one year later she received a second honorary degree from the University of California itself. She was an early woman pioneer in the building of the intellectual and institutional foundations of modern social welfare. To her, social research and social reform were complementary forces in achieving social change.[57]

Peixotto's students saw her as a charismatic and elegantly groomed authority figure, "crisp, theoretical, and academic," with no "chummy relationship" with her students.[58] She did not marry or have children, a fact she described in a university form requesting her marital status and number of children as "opportunities missed." She lived with her mother near campus; the two were described by a contemporary as "a scholarly daughter and an admiring mother who was pleased that the daughter had recognition on campus."[59] To faculty she was a liberal, caring, intelligent person.[60] Although she was the first female to hold a full professorship at Berkeley, in 1918, neither she nor Lucy Sprague attended faculty meetings. Lucy Sprague explained, "Certainly we could have come, but I know that it would have prejudiced the men against us, and we already had enough prejudices to live down."[61] In several letters to President Wheeler, a personal friend, Peixotto complained about the demeaning treatment she received and also about the failure of the university to appoint any men to the department of social economics. She wrote:

> It has been mortifying enough these past weeks to face that when it is a question of promotions in our department, I am invariably the last to get any evidence of merit. Later comers get first place. . . . When to this criticism the fact is added that, after what I thought a thorough understanding with Dr. Plehn, neither Mr. Black nor any other in his place is to be appointed to social economics. . . then I feel it is unavoidably my duty to bring the matter to your attention. The work on social economics has in four years grown from a mere handful

of students to some 230 last year. . . . I can never carry it alone—can never again give thirteen hours of instruction. The results are not merely bad physically but are intellectually stultifying.[62]

In 1934, in an essay written honoring Peixotto on the occasion of her retirement, Professor Hatfield insisted that her academic prowess had not been inconsistent with the traditional female role:

It may not be inappropriate to mention another public service, of an altogether different type. There have been, and perhaps still are, some benighted males who have the delusion that high intellectual attainments and a life of professional and public service are incompatible with what used to be considered the essential feminine attributes. Homage should therefore be paid to one who combines all the intellectual qualities of the dowdiest of bluestockings with the distinction and charm of the polished hostess and the gracious lady. To prove the possibility of such a combination is a real service to society.[63]

In 1909 Wheeler appointed Peixotto to chair the Domestic Science Committee. She invested her efforts in introducing students to social movements outside the university and to providing them with the skills and knowledge necessary to participate actively and professionally in social reform.

Lucy Sprague, like her colleague and close friend, Peixotto, looked to home economics to open new professional avenues for women. She had grown up the fourth of six children in a wealthy Chicago merchant family; her father's wholesale grocery business was, at one point, the largest of its kind in the world. She was a very shy, introspective, lonely, and extremely sensitive child, tutored at home like her brothers and sisters. She read her way through her father's huge library. As a teenager, through her father's connections, she met Jane Addams of the Hull House; John Dewey of the university's Laboratory School; and Alice Freeman Palmer, former president of Wellesley College, who with her husband, George Herbert Palmer, the noted Harvard philosopher, treated Lucy as the daughter they did not have.[64] Through these leaders of reform and education Lucy Sprague was introduced to women at the university, such as Marion Talbot and

Sophonisba Breckinridge, who were influential in Progressive Era social reform movements and in the advancement of women in higher education.

At fifteen Lucy Sprague moved with her parents to southern California, where she served for a while as nurse to an ailing family. For two years after that she attended a high school in Los Angeles, and resisting her family's wishes that she come home "for good,"[65] she accepted an invitation from Alice and George Palmer to live with them in Cambridge, Massachusetts, and attend Radcliffe College. Rebelling against her father, in particular, she enrolled at Radcliffe in 1896 at eighteen, graduating with honors in philosophy four years later.

After graduation Sprague returned to California and resumed the role of family nurse, only to be rescued a second time by the Palmers, who took her with them to Europe. Alice Palmer died unexpectedly while they were in Paris, and Lucy returned to Cambridge with the distraught widower. She cared for him there for several years, while taking some graduate courses at Harvard and working as secretary to Radcliffe's dean.

In 1903 University of California President Wheeler, a close friend of the Palmers and of Lucy's brother-in-law, offered her a job working with women students, prelude to a position of dean of women. She accepted appointments as a reader in economics and in English, and after three years, she was appointed both dean of women and assistant professor of English. With Peixotto she was one of the first women to hold a regular faculty position at the University of California.

Contrary to the expectation of many Berkeley faculty, Lucy Sprague did not view her new role as dean as a "warden of women, sedate and motherly," who would "supervise the mixed boarding houses and keep down the scandals on campus." She saw her job as expanding the educational, professional, and social opportunities of Berkeley's women students.[66] She advised the first-year students on courses, approved their study lists, taught sex education courses, worked to strengthen women students' organizations, and, in particular, attempted to improve women students' housing conditions. During her first year as dean, she investigated every home and boarding house where women students lived and visited every student club.

In a survey of first-year women students, Sprague learned that 80.5 percent of 252 were at Berkeley for a teacher's certificate.[67] The fact that teacher training was the only professional training the university offered to women she found troubling, convinced that "a university should be more than a normal school," as teacher's colleges were then called.[68] In consequence, she sought to introduce programs to Berkeley that would extend the range of career possibilities for women: home economics, library science, nursing, and social charity. She was remembered by her Berkeley colleagues and women students as a powerful and stunning figure, "tall and beautiful, dressing in long skirts and embroidered blouses, wearing silver chains or intricate beads and a velvet band around her neck, the thick hair piled on top of her head."[69]

Jessica Peixotto and Lucy Sprague lived together for one year. Like her friend, Lucy Sprague was concerned that there was "nothing in the university to tempt the women students' interest in civic affairs,"[70] and she tried to remedy the lack by taking students on field trips to a baby health center, a settlement house, an orphanage, the county poorhouse, and the docks. She opened her home at Berkeley once a week to women students for poetry reading and refreshments. One outcome of these readings, in 1911, was an open-air pageant or masque, the *Parthenia*, planned, written, and executed by the more than 1,200 women students. It was to become an annual event, one that Sprague thought gave the women some standing in their own eyes and in the eyes of the rest of the campus. Until then, "as a group, the women students contributed nothing to university life."[71]

Sprague spent four months in New York in 1911 working with noted pioneers in the development of women's professions, who together represented a broad spectrum of modern social welfare methods. Among them were Lillian Ward, director and founder of the Henry Street Settlement; Florence Kelley, national secretary of the Consumers League; Mary Richmond, head of the Charity Organization Society of the Russell Sage Foundation; Pauline Goldmark, research analyst for the Russell Sage Foundation; and Julia Richman, a district superintendent in the New York public schools.

Back in California, in 1912, Sprague resigned as dean, married the famous Berkeley economics professor Wesley Clair Mitchell, and moved to New York. She raised four children there and some years later established the Bureau of Educational Experiment, a private educational corporation for teaching and researching progressive education and educational experiments, a forerunner of the Bank Street College of Education. Over her lifetime, Sprague Mitchell wrote, co-authored, or edited six books for adults and twenty for children, and after her husband's death in 1948, she continued to work at Bank Street for eight more years, then moved back to Palo Alto, to be near one of her children. As with many of the pioneers in women's education, not until late in her life, at eighty years old, was she honored by the academic world for her many accomplishments. In 1956 she received the Radcliffe Graduate Chapter Medal for Distinguished Achievements, and in 1958 she received an honorary doctoral degree, the LL.D., from the University of California.

Indeed, Lucy Sprague supported the establishment of home economics not only as a way to increase career options for women, to introduce and engage women students in social reform movements, but also as a "bargaining chip" with the president in her campaign to improve women's position on campus. Half of the women students lived at home, and half lived with relatives or in boarding houses. She suggested a dormitory system as "the best unifying force and easiest and most natural way of establishing social standards,"[72] linking her plan with President Wheeler's "pet ideas" of a home economics program for women where they could gain "experience in housekeeping."

Following in Lucy Sprague's footsteps, the second dean of women at Berkeley, Lucy Ward Stebbins, was also concerned that women be trained for fields other than teaching, "more than merely the training of technical teachers for secondary schools." Stebbins, a 1902 graduate of Radcliffe, was two years younger than Lucy Sprague. The two women knew each other at Radcliffe. Lucy Ward Stebbins was a lecturer on charities in the Department of Economics and served as assistant to Dean Sprague for two years before she succeeded her in the fall of 1912. During Stebbins' years as assistant dean of women, President Wheeler refused to pay her a salary, forcing Lucy Sprague to pay her out of Sprague's own pocket.

A native Californian, Lucy Ward Stebbins was born in San

Francisco in 1880. Her father, Dr. Horatio Stebbins, a well-known pastor of the First Unitarian Church of San Francisco, was one of the founders of the College of California, the institution that made a state university in California possible. In fact, Dr. Stebbins was one of the nominees for first president of the University of California, and he served on the board of regents from its beginning in 1868 until 1893, a period of some twenty-five years.[73] For Lucy Stebbins the university was a well-known entity both because of her father's involvement and because she was a student there for a short time before transferring to Radcliffe.

Unlike her predecessor, Stebbins came to her work as dean of women with prior administrative experience. After graduation from Radcliffe she worked for two years as secretary to the dean of Radcliffe College. Then, from 1904 through 1908, she was general secretary for the Boston Society for the Care of Girls and from 1908 through 1910, she was district secretary for the Boston Associated Charities.

When Lucy Sprague resigned, Lucy Stebbins was appointed dean of women and assistant professor of social economy. She became an associate professor in 1917 and professor of social economics in 1924. She held these titles until her resignation in 1941, when she became professor of social economics emeritus. In 1933, Mills College conferred an honorary doctoral degree, the LL.D., upon her. Stebbins was described as lovely, but very businesslike. She was seen as concerned about women students, but remote. Mary Blossom Davidson, her assistant for many years, described her as an intellectual person.[74]

Unlike Lucy Sprague, Lucy Stebbins never established a close relationship with the Wheelers or with any of the following presidents. Her position on home economics seems to be similar to that held by the ACA, of which she was a member. From 1912 through 1916, Stebbins continued in the same direction as Lucy Sprague, working on women's housing issues, vocational information guidelines, and community and identity building. She appealed to the administration to offer home economics courses that would include professional work in a graduate school. Home economics, she was convinced, would focus the academic career of women "who have no special gift or inclination and fall aimlessly into the curriculum of the colleges of social and natural sciences."[75] A school of home economics would offer a choice to women graduate students. "More and more frequently," Stebbins wrote, "young women say to me: We do not want to teach and we must earn our living. What can we do?"[76]

A "WOMEN'S DEPARTMENT": A FORM OF SEGREGATION?

President Wheeler countered Lucy Ward Stebbins's proposals for a school of home economics with a proposal not for a school, but for a department within the College of Letters and Science, with under-graduate courses only. His plan for courses in domestic art and domestic science narrowed the field of home economics to design and applied nutrition, as a possible substitute for the traditional liberal arts education. It would bring two previously unrelated subjects into one department and thus combine all course offerings explicitly designed for women students into a single organizational unit.[77] The Committee on Domestic Sciences, chaired by Dr. Peixotto, vehemently opposed Wheeler's idea for creating a "woman's department," seeing it as female segregation. They expressed concern that the merging of these two subjects into one undergraduate department instead of establishing a graduate school would reduce its academic status. They warned the president that "the university should not aim to give women a technique guaranteed to equip them for all the emergencies of home keeping."

The University Council of the deans of colleges and the heads of the departments, after a discussion of the recommendations of the Committee of Domestic Science, indicated that the best place for home economics would be within the School of Education, only to learn from President Wheeler that the university's regents had already accepted his own proposal for a united Department of Home Economics in the College of Letters and Science. Home economics at Berkeley thus was established autocratically in 1916 with little support from women faculty and women students, let alone the University Council itself. A separate sphere for women students at Berkeley had been created, as Dr. Peixotto's committee had feared, pooling the women together and separating them from men within the supposedly coeducational institution (see figure 4). By adding home economics to the traditional curriculum, the administration was freed from the necessity of integrating women's interests and needs into universitywide offerings. Furthermore, a general undergraduate home economics major in the College of Letters and Science, as a substitute for the general liberal arts curriculum, required little institutional support and was easily accommodated within the established academic setting

Figure 4. University of California class of 1917, Department of Household Science (Author's private collection)

without much impact on the traditional curriculum. Also, to locate home economics in the School of Education as the University Council had suggested would have led women even more into the teaching profession, among other things, increasing the number of women who might remain single, outside of motherhood, in President Wheeler's eyes, reinforcing a "social evil" he had made it his mission to forestall.

Creating a School of Home Economics as Peixotto, Sprague, and Stebbins wanted, would have required serious institutional commitment to specialized graduate work and professional training based on research, more expensive to maintain and requiring larger research allocations and more space.

A Department (not a school) of Home Economics at Berkeley was an administrative response typical of public coeducational universities in general to the rising number of women college students at the turn of the century. Historian Harold Wechsler's definition of "group repulsion" would apply to Berkeley's behavior. Wechsler has found segregation to be systematically applied to any identifiable new and previously excluded student group as it enters American higher education: poor students, women, Jews, and blacks.[78] A home economics department was typical also of strategies employed by women inside and outside the university to broaden the next generation of women's career opportunities and to employ the concepts and methods of science to ameliorate the social conditions inside and outside the home.

Historians of education have offered several explanations for the introduction of home economics into colleges and universities. Frederick Rudolph believes that American land-grant colleges and universities introduced home economics "as counterparts to the vocational programs considered appropriate for men."[79] Laurence Veysey attributes it to the utilitarian reform ideals of post–Civil War America, particularly of the Progressive Era of 1890 to 1915, of democracy, serviceability, and pragmatism, when colleges and universities were expected to work toward practical social benefits and render service to the state. "Very quickly the serviceable university began to usher in a discordant variety of new departments of learning," Veysey writes. "Such untraditional disciplines as pedagogy, domestic science, business administration, sanitary science, physical education, and various kinds of engineering were all becoming firmly established at a number of leading universities by the turn of the century."[80] His explanation comes closest to the intention Berkeley women faculty cited for introducing home economics into the University of California.

Sociologist Linda Marie Fritschner finds that midwestern coeducational land-grant colleges and universities introduced home economics as "a backward-looking response to social change; an attempt to resist trends in female employment and restore traditional values."[81] She refutes technical-functional argumentation postulating a direct relationship between educational expansion and occupational expansion as applicable to women's education.[82] Her rationale might explain the Berkeley administration's eagerness to introduce an undergraduate liberal arts home economics program.

Barbara Solomon, a historian of women's education, emphasizes the many scientific advances at the turn of the century and the consequent changes in the labor market: "Scientific developments in the increasingly industrialized society not only created new demands for the university training of professional men but generated needs in service fields that trained women could fill."[83] Although her explanation, like that of technical-functional theorists, relates modernization to the changed occupational sector and to women's education, she sees the occupational sector for women as stratified, maintaining that women, unlike men, get academic training for only a small sector of the labor market—the service sector—one not only constricted but characterized by low pay, low mobility, and low status.

The creation of the undergraduate department of home economics at Berkeley can best be understood, I have concluded, as an administrative strategy to isolate the many women students enrolling in the College of Letters and Science and to minimize their competition with men, while at the same time preparing them for what was seen as their appropriate vocation as wives and mothers. The promotion of home economics as a new academic discipline by women inside and outside the university, on the other hand, was undertaken with a goal of broadening women's sphere and employment opportunities. It was their tragedy that, while the support for home economics they had built up was exploited, the ultimate result was a travesty of their aims.

Chapter 2

University Schooling for "the Housekeeper, Homemaker, and Mother"

The Department of Home Economics at Berkeley was established through a long, painful process. Neither the Committee on Home Economics nor the first faculty member hired to establish it had any real power, and the lack of power dragged out the implementation process. Muddled authority lines confused the faculty involved, who only too late realized that they had been played off against each other. Gender influenced every decision about home economics President Wheeler made.

After seven years of proposals and a tug-of-war between the president and the Committee on Domestic Science over organizational structure and choice of faculty, the Department of Home Economics emerged in 1916 with an undergraduate liberal arts program in the College of Letters and Science.

In 1909 President Wheeler set up the Committee on Domestic

Science and charged it with designing a curriculum for home economics at Berkeley. He appointed Jessica Peixotto, then assistant professor of sociology in the Department of Economics, to chair the committee. Other members were William C. Hays, assistant professor of architecture; Charles Hyde, professor of sanitary engineering; Meyer Jaffa, professor of nutrition; Eugen Neuhaus, assistant professor of decorative design; and starting in 1913, Lucy Stebbins, dean of women.

The appointed faculty members came from areas that home economics, in its subfields, embraced. William Hays was brought in also to represent the element of "shelter" in the home economics curriculum. He had come to Berkeley in 1904 on the invitation of the campus architect, John Galen Howard, and opened an office in San Francisco as well as taught in the College of Architecture. Charles Hyde, who joined the Berkeley faculty in 1905 as assistant professor, an M.I.T. graduate in sanitary engineering and a full professor at age thirty-four though he had only a bachelor's degree, was to introduce sanitation to home economics. The Berkeley program in sanitary engineering proudly claimed to be the first of its kind in the western United States. He pioneered environmental issues, as many home economists did also in the context of their concerns about purity of drinking water and pollution of rivers. Meyer Jaffa, at fifty-two the oldest member of the committee, a specialist in nutrition and a "pioneer in the pure food movement,"[1] at the time of his appointment was both professor of nutrition and the director of the California State Bureau of Food and Drugs. Eugen Neuhaus was assistant professor of decorative design at the San Francisco Institute of Art, then affiliated with the University of California. He taught simultaneously at Berkeley in the Department of Drawing, which comprised engineering drawing, architectural drawing, and drawing from the antique.

There were only two women members, and one of them, Jessica Peixotto, the chair, was the only member who had earned a Ph.D. At age forty-two she was the second oldest member of the committee, and yet was still an assistant professor. Lucy Stebbins was appointed to the committee in her role as dean of women after Lucy Sprague had resigned from this post to marry Wesley Mitchell, a Berkeley economics professor, and moved to New York to resume work in the education of children. Stebbins was, like

Peixotto, an assistant professor in economics. As an economist she was interested in the field of home economics because it was involved in developing and teaching the methods necessary for social reforms.

In a letter to professor Meyer Jaffa of nutrition, in the College of Agriculture, President Wheeler explained the committee's mission, to give young women "something better to do than . . . more and more courses in English":

> I want you to act on a committee, of which Miss Peixotto will be the chairman, for the making up of a body to constitute a sort of curriculum in domestic science. I believe that there are courses already offered in this University almost sufficient to make up a body of studies that could be called a curriculum. We do not wish to have in the University, of course, the actual teaching of the handicrafts—that belongs in the high school, the trade school, and possibly the normal school. But we have a great duty to meet, it seems to me, in giving the young women who swarm into our University something better to do than this piling up of more and ever more courses in English, as is the futile tendency of the day.[2]

President Wheeler seems to have had a limited solution in mind: a program to pull together from existing sources, a plan that would not demand extensive financial expenditures or administrative time.

Jaffa, in a letter congratulating Wheeler for his efforts and thanking him for the privilege of working on this committee, pointed to his own view of women's education. It did not conflict with Wheeler's own: "We do not want the teaching of the handicrafts, but I should like to see women students, each and every one of them, prepared intellectually to meet and master the problems that confront the housekeeper, home maker and mother."[3]

The Frustrating Struggle for Faculty and Status as a School

For nearly two years thereafter, things were quiet. There was no correspondence between the president and the committee on the matter nor any mention of home economics in the student newspaper. Then, in May 1911, the Committee on Domestic Science sent a report to President Wheeler informing him that it had "worked out a curriculum which seems to be pretty well met by courses given in the various departments in the University, with the exception of a department in Textiles and Decorative Arts."[4] Accordingly, the chair, Professor Jessica Peixotto, began to search for a qualified person to teach both of these new areas.

For the teaching of textiles John Galen Howard, professor of architecture and the university architect responsible for implementing the Berkeley campus plan (designed by the French architect Henri Bénard), recommended Mary Lois Kissell, a Columbia University graduate.[5] Mary Kissell, known as an expert in the history of textiles, embroidery, and primitive weaving, had a master's degree from the School of Household Arts. At first, she rejected the offer because she was in the process of completing a book. But she said that she would be available the following year. In 1912 she accepted the offer and came to Berkeley as associate professor of domestic art, with an annual salary of $2,400 and an additional $500 for equipment, a salary comparable to that of men at the associate professor entry level. (Five hundred dollars was too little for slides, illustrations, and art books, she said, and she offered to make her own books and materials available to students, if the university would pay the shipping costs. This was arranged.)

Mary Kissell brought to her new post five years of research experience in primitive textiles at the American Museum for Natural History in New York and five months of special study of historical textiles abroad. She had gained a reputation as an unusual woman. The Baltimore *Evening Sun* referred to her "wandering alone in the wilds with nothing to defend herself" when she studied weaving methods of native Americans in Arizona. "Mary Lois Kissell, noted authority on Textiles, will go to California," said the picture caption. "With an Indian woman interpreter, she rode her pony through the wildest sections of the country, gathering specimens of clothing, basketry, weaving in general and the various things that the savage tribes use for personal adornment. Miss Kissell adopted the garb of the Southwest, but carried no revolver." Her report of this field trip "is considered of the greatest value in that it shows the presence of the same motifs in the weaving of the Indians as those which appear in the more elaborate rugs and carpets of Persia and China."[6]

Kissell was eager to meet the challenge. "I am anticipating the work with great enthusiasm as the opportunity seems ideal in the broadness of its scope, in this the added knowledge that I shall instruct under an appreciative and considerate executive [President Wheeler]," she wrote. "Under such conditions and entrusted with such responsibilities, can one do less than the best?"[7] Charmed by Berkeley, she wrote shortly after her arrival, "The genial spirit which pervades the University of California is inspiring and has caught me in its spell."[8]

Kissell stayed in constant contact with Peixotto. They both agreed that the new courses in textiles should be research courses and thus upper division courses. During her first semester in fall 1912, Kissell taught four upper division courses, two in textiles and two in household design.

The University Catalogue of 1912 and 1913 describes the courses:

Textiles 101A. "The characteristics, distribution, and use of textile raw materials—cotton, flax, wool and silk; and the process of manufacture—spinning, weaving, dyeing, finishing."

Textiles 101B. "Fabrics—an intensive study of materials with the aid of the microscope, chemical and physical tests; analysis of pattern; applied decoration; economic and artistic use."

Household Design of Primitive People 102A. "A study of the principles of design used by peoples of lower culture."

Household Design in Modern Houses 102B. "A consideration of the principles of fine art as applied to house furnishing together with the aesthetic and economic use of fabrics, wool, clay, and metal."

The October 12, 1912, issue of *The Daily Californian* reported, "It is welcome news to the women interested along these lines that California is to have at last a College of Domestic Arts and Sciences, and it is hoped that funds will soon be donated for the new building and for carrying on the work so that next year it will be possible for those wishing to specialize in home economics to do so. There is no reason why we should not have here in the West, in time, as great a department as Columbia has in the East."[9]

Mary Kissell held the same opinion about the department's goals and, in November 1912, asked President Wheeler, with Professor Pcixotto, to arrange for someone to be appointed to teach a course in household design so she could use her time "for the growth of home economics."[10] The administration refused her request, and the following semester, spring 1913, she taught four courses once again. But at the end of her second semester, Kissell threatened to leave unless two additional faculty in domestic art and domestic science were appointed for the next semester.[11] Wheeler responded positively this time, but only after the Committee on Home Economics also recommended that Wheeler appoint the two new faculty. Kissell then set out on a recruiting tour to home economics departments in thirteen major universities and colleges in the East and Midwest.[12]

On the advice of the vice president of the American Home Economics Association, Dr. Langsworthy of the U.S. Agricultural Station in Washington, D.C., Kissell recommended for the household science position two women with Ph.D.s in chemistry, with experience in the field of household science and in administration.[13]

However, the two indicated that they would be willing to leave their present positions for the move to California only with an agreed-upon promotion to full professorship during the second year and with a salary comparable to those they already received— according to Professor Kissell's letter, both of the candidates already earned above $2,400. Each also said she must be put in charge of foods instruction.[14] The maximum the administration was willing to pay was $2,400 and that for only one position,[15] and it categorically refused any advance commitment for promotion. Therefore, the university's opportunity to build a department with a core of experienced women was lost.

Kissell made an alternative suggestion, to appoint two recent master's students from Columbia University, but this proposal also was rejected, this time by a member of the Committee on Domestic Science, Professor Meyer Jaffa of nutrition, who had become secretary of the Committee on Domestic Science in 1913. It was under his administration that the committee changed its name to the Committee on Home Economics as home economics is "roughly inclusive and of nation-wide use."[16] He was the one who had supported publicly Wheeler's rationale for preparing women students, as Jaffa put it four years earlier, "to meet and master the problems that confront the house keeper, home maker and mother."[17] Professor Jaffa now proposed a cheaper solution—to hire the person who had been instructor for home economics in the summer session, a Miss Davis, a former high school teacher of domestic science. Jaffa vouched for her, noting that "her scientific foundation is good and adequate" and "we are all impressed by her personality."[18] Hired on a temporary basis as a lecturer in dietetics for the fall 1913 semester was Professor Jaffa's own wife, Adelle Jaffa, a physician, with no university or other teaching experience.[19]

Professor Kissell's search for the second person, an experienced, academically oriented domestic art teacher, was also unsuccessful, this time because she could find no "strong women in this work with a University viewpoint."[20] As she did the year before, Mary Kissell again taught four courses each semester during the 1913 through 1914 academic year.

The appointment of Dr. Adelle Jaffa was surprising. Mrs. Jaffa was the mother of two small children. Her lectureship lasted for only one semester; President Wheeler then terminated it. Dr. Jaffa wrote to President Wheeler that she wanted to make sure that he understood that his decision neither "hurt nor disappointed her." She told him that she had been debating whether or not to resign because of the "conflict between the strongly centered and personal motherhood and the broader and impersonal [work]."[21] She had accepted the work only because she felt she could help to get the home economics department organized; the women students with an interest in the new field needed someone to teach "applied dietetics," "feeding infants and children," and "modern theories of disease in relation to diet."[22] She closed her letter saying, "So you see, you have made it easier for me. You have relieved me of the necessity of closing the door with my own hand and shutting myself out from work I love to do!" Wheeler replied, "That's the right spirit."[23]

Left alone with no help in building up home economics, Kissell wrote a blunt report to Wheeler in mid-January 1914 about the state of home economics at the university and the work accomplished during the department's first one-and-one-half years.

At present the University is doing little or nothing in Home Economics study for better home making, for teaching, or research work. The little that is being done is in a disorganized shape. I believe the University of California could and should have a great School of Home Economics, independent of any school or department now present on the campus, and this school should be divided under its natural divisions—Food, Clothing, Housing, Household Administration and Household Education—into five departments, each headed by the strongest and best equipped women in the country.[24]

Her report outlined in detail these five "natural dimensions" of home economics—food, clothing, housing, household administration, and household education—each of which should form separate departments in a school of home economics. She proposed that such a school of home economics have its own building with laboratories, a museum, and an exhibition space. It must be headed by "someone to unify the work and to organize and relate the courses with an eye to the general scope of the work."[25] She herself intended to retreat totally from all organizational work and to devote herself entirely to teaching three courses each semester and doing research on textile work during the next year, because "no one has the strength to carry both teaching and organizing successfully under present conditions."

If President Wheeler ever made a response to Mary Kissell's request, none has been found in the archives. All that exists is a letter from the president to the Committee on Home Economics asking for recommendations for further developments for instruction, for an outline of the different branches that ought to be taught, and for a statement of the distribution of the work among different departments.[26] If he did address the committee alone, he disregarded Professor Kissell.

Kissell had expected to work well with President Wheeler, having seen him originally as "appreciative and considerate." And, as she had written to him only one month earlier, in December 1913: "It is pleasant indeed to be where the possibilities for the work are so great and where so much confidence is entrusted in one. I certainly appreciate your confidence in me, a confidence which I trust may not only be kept but increased."[27]

Yet now, for the second time, her requests were apparently rejected. First, during the summer, every recommendation she put forth for qualified women to fill appointments in domestic science—women with Ph.D.s and administrative skills—was refused. Now she had received no response to a major report, if the records can be trusted. President Wheeler seemed to have played the Committee on Home Economics off against Professor Kissell and *vice versa*.

Six months earlier, in April 1913, the Committee on Home Economics had presented to President Wheeler a report on the "most urgent needs for the academic year 1913–14."[28] He had responded that he was waiting for Mary Kissell's recommendations following her trip to the East and Midwest. She made her recommendations, but nothing happened for another semester, except the brief appointment of Professor Jaffa's wife. Now, in January 1914, the reverse was occurring. The president turned to the committee on home economics for its recommendations and ignored those Kissell had presented. The president's behavior had two effects: first, it muddled the authority relationship between the committee and Mary Kissell, with neither the committee nor Mary Kissell knowing clearly who was held as the authority on home economics. Second, it pitted the two proponents for home economics against each other. In addition, the collaboration between Professor Kissell and the committee, which had functioned well until then, was now undermined. In January 1914 Kissell complained to Wheeler about the committee: "The greatest trouble seems to come from the number of people who are trying to help in the work but who know nothing about it, although they think they do."[29] She believed the Home Economics Committee wanted to place home economics in the College of Agriculture. She stopped going to committee meetings altogether.

On February 3, 1914, frustrated and disappointed about the discrepancy between the administration's verbal commitments to home economics, its circumvention of departmental responses for faculty, and its refusal of financial support, Mary Kissell resigned. It was two weeks after she had delivered her comprehensive report to the president's office. In her resignation letter to President Wheeler, Kissell noted that she was a cause of "some disruption" and that "money and strength," without which a respected school of home economics could not exist, "were two hard things to find." She had not found them at Berkeley.

I seem to be a thorn in the flesh and to be causing some disruption on the campus, so this morning I sent in to Mr. Henderson my resignation. I cannot think of hindering in the least the development here of home economics, therefore my decision. My personal plans are rapidly maturing, I sail early in May for a year of research abroad.

Home economics work in the University of California seems naturally, at this time, to pass into the College of Agriculture, since they have the funds for its support. However, home conditions on the farms of the state are far better than those in our urban communities and in these last there are many times the homes than in the former. For this reason Berkeley seemed to me the one place in the country where home economics could have its broadest development, reaching both farm and city conditions and sending its message through well trained teachers.

Dean Baily said last summer that Cornell knew that home economics did not belong in the Agricultural department, that it should be a school in itself, but since no other department in Cornell would mother this child, the Agricultural department had to. The home economics work at Cornell has an agricultural stamp, just as that at Columbia is biased by its pedagogical setting.

So we have in our universities of the land a one sided development in home economics, which it appeared to me might be avoided in the University of California. This seemed the institution to establish a school of home economics on broad scientific, economic and artistic lines, with interests of the state considered. But of course this would cost money and strength, two hard things to find.[30]

The administration had in mind no school like that put forward by Kissell, only a department, and Kissell's resignation was accepted. A confidential note from President Wheeler to the dean of the College of Agriculture about her resignation shows how correctly Kissell had evaluated the administration's attitude. "I think she is an intense and nervous person who takes some things unnecessarily seriously," Wheeler wrote. "We must however, of course, be careful to adjust as clearly as we can the departmental frontier."[31]

President Wheeler's official letter accepting her resignation was cast in an entirely different tone.

> I was very sorry to receive your letter of February third. . . . I cannot believe that it is best that Home Economics should be as a department made a part of the College of Agriculture, and I had not supposed that anyone in the university wanted it so. I am sure we shall all regret your decision to withdraw from the university but shall always feel thankful to you for the great stimulus you have given to studies in your chosen field and the excellent foundations you have laid here."[32]

The administration had yet several other hurdles to climb before reaching its goal of a departmental structure for home economics. Now, it was the Committee of Home Economics that was urging the establishment of a school.

Developing an Organizational Structure

On March 4, 1914, the Committee on Home Economics presented its version of a plan for "status, needs, organization, and administration of Home Economics in the University."[33] It began by referring to the disagreement on the structural organization of home economics to which Mary Lois Kissell's resignation letter alluded, but without citing it directly.

> In view of the very apparent lack of crystallization of opinion with respect to the needs, scope of effort, and organization of work in the university with respect to that field which, following precedent, has somewhat unsatisfactorily been designated 'Home Economics,' the committee desires to advance certain propositions which appear to us to be basic and necessary to the effective solution of the problems involved.

It was obvious that already, at this early stage, Berkeley faculty were dissatisfied with the title *home economics* for the new area of study.

The committee plan outlined resembled, at many points, Professor Kissell's own recommendations. It strongly objected to a departmental structure and proposed instead a professional school of home economics, "because no other structure would allow for broad scale offerings and could house different types of home economics programs." Only a school would be a large enough organizational unit, with its own dean with direct access to the president, its own budget, and its own Ph.D. program. It cited as existing prototypes at Berkeley the schools of architecture, education, and jurisprudence. It urged the university, as Mary Kissell had done, to "seek among its friends for funds with which to build and equip a structure to house all the interests in home economics." Its proposal referred to three potential student clienteles rather than different areas within home economics as Kissell had used: (1) those who would make future instruction in home economics their vocation; (2) those who planned to enter home economics-related businesses such as management of apartments, houses, restaurants, interior decorating services, and the like; and (3) future homemakers.

The committee urged that a person heading this school should be appointed immediately and given "adequate and reasonable power." It proposed that, at least for the next two years, this individual should be chosen from among present Berkeley faculty. It recommended that two associate professors and two instructors, in domestic art and in nutrition, be hired immediately. Attached to the committee's plan was a five-year general curriculum for home economics; it was the first printed document outlining a home economics curriculum. It was designed for students majoring in foods, housing, or clothing.

Interestingly, an earlier, unsigned draft of this report found among the university files had passages written in far stronger language. This draft criticized the administration for delaying the organization of home economics and for setting up a "hydra-headed" structure—the Committee on Home Economics—which controlled an academic program, while denying power to the person actually running the program. This discarded draft stated forcefully:

> All human history demonstrated that "No man can serve two masters"; in other words, that divided authority cannot produce or evolve effective administration or comprehensive and co-ordinated organization. . . . It is painfully evident that the

work outlined above cannot be organized or effectively administrated under the present irrational and haphazard policy of committee control. Without regard of the personal fitness of the individuals composing the present committee and notwithstanding their generous and honest desire to advance the interests of the work in the best and largest way, such a scheme is inherently inadequate and ineffectual and is excusable only as a temporary expedient. In behalf of the existing committee it is believed that it may truthfully be said that no example of effective results *under similar conditions* of committee control [over an academic program] can be cited in this or any other University.[34]

Apparently, this critique never formally reached President Wheeler. The milder, more conciliatory report of March 4 did. Despite the committee's diplomacy, however, the judicious recommendations did not meet with the president's approval. In a short note to David Barrows, then dean of faculties, to whom Wheeler had delegated all dealings on home economics, the president stated that "the oversight of the course should remain in the hands of the committee as at present, unless Professor Hyde can undertake it."[35] Wheeler did agree to hire two new faculty, but he gave no word about a possible structure for the new field. He ended his note to Barrows, "I should like to have you go ahead and settle all this."[36]

"WOMEN CANNOT TAKE RESPONSIBILITY AS WELL AS MEN . . ."

There seem to be three possible reasons for President Wheeler's refusal to accept both Mary Kissell's and the committee's recommendations. One is the fact that both proposals assumed that one function of home economics was to prepare women for work outside the home. This would have gone beyond Wheeler's philosophy of preparing women students simply to become wives and mothers. A second is the fact that both proposed a school, not a department, as the appropriate organizational structure. President Wheeler wanted something small, inexpensive, and effortless to construct. To build a school along the lines of the schools of architecture or law, as the committee had recommended, would mean considerable allocation of finances and administrative time, two things which, as Kissell said, were "hard to find." A third reason could have been that President Wheeler could not envision a woman administering an entire school with its own budget and with direct access to the president. His opinion about women and their ability to do business was, indeed, quite devastating: "Women cannot take responsibility as well as men can because they do not trust their own judgment."[37]

Charles Hyde, the person Wheeler wanted to oversee the developing home economics department, was a full professor of sanitary engineering and a member of the Home Economics Committee; while Jessica Peixotto, who had been chair of the Home Economics Committee for five years, was still an assistant professor. Hyde had become a full professor at age thirty-four with only a B.A., while Peixotto, with a Ph.D., had remained an instructor for three years before becoming an assistant professor. For Wheeler, gender mattered, both in promotions and in authority. Either a man should head the new program, or the entire committee should, but not a woman.

With home economics still in the hands of the dean of faculties, David Barrows, the implementation process took yet another turn. He presented the latest report of the Committee on Home Economics to the University Council, the standing committee of the Academic Senate. The council came up with a new idea, that home economics be administered by the School of Education since it included the training of teachers.[38] Richard Boone, acting director of the School of Education, responded that the school "would gladly assume responsibility" for all "Upper Division and Graduate courses" of home economics.[39] The Committee on Home Economics did not consider this a solution, and, on September 9, 1914, it succeeded in convincing the University Council to recommend to the Academic Senate:

1. That a college of Home Economics be established.

2. That the proposed college should have a dean or other executive officer provided as soon as possible.

3. That for the purpose of organization the first four years of the course outlined by the Committee on Home Economics be adopted as a provisional curriculum for the proposed college.[40]

On December 8, 1914, the Board of Regents approved the plan.[41] The path seemed cleared for a School of Home Economics at Berkeley despite President Wheeler's consistent opposition. Or so it seemed. The board had not counted on the president's continuing to press for his own preference.

In the meantime, Lucy Stebbins, dean of women, had been dispatched to the East Coast to search both for a successor for Mary L. Kissell in household art and for a person to teach household science. The idea of hiring a person from the Berkeley campus was obviously, by now, abandoned. Her first choice for the assistant professor position in domestic art, a candidate from the Pratt Institute in New York, requested a salary of $2,500 and was rejected by the administration. There was now no one to fill the vacancy left by Kissell before the fall semester started; whereupon a graduate from the Providence School of Design, Mary Patterson, was hired as assistant professor of domestic art at $2,000, which was $400 less than Kissell's salary. In August, Lucy Ward Stebbins found a person to fill the position for household science: Agnes Fay Morgan, a Ph.D. in chemistry from the University of Chicago. The Board of Regents promptly approved her appointment as assistant professor of nutrition in the College of Agriculture at a salary of $1,800, starting January 1, 1915[42] (see figure 5).

Mary Patterson, at forty-two,[43] apparently had no prior administrative experience, nor was she astute in organizational matters, judging from the tone of her letters and her later activities on campus (see figure 6). Her family was educated and upper-middle class; her father had a law degree from Harvard, and her mother had been educated in a women's religious school in Boston. She herself had been taught by tutors and governesses until she was ten. Then she had attended the Lincoln School in Providence until she was seventeen. After a decade of practical experience in business and teaching, as she put it in the university's biographical records, she earned a degree from the Rhode Island School of Design and took summer classes at Harvard on the theory of design and color. After graduation in 1905, she received a postgraduate fellowship and studied for a year in Europe. A person of utmost politeness, at times with a tone of submissiveness and insecurity in her communications, she was a woman with characteristics almost polar opposite to those of Mary Kissell. She was a member of several

Figure 5. First meeting of Home Economics Division of the Land Grant College Association, in Berkeley, California, 1915 (Author's private collection)

Figure 6. Mary Frances Patterson, associate professor of decorative art and design, 1914–1943, department of household art 1918–1939 (photo 1936) (University of California Archives)

cultural societies and women's clubs: the Shakespearian Society, the American Federation of Arts, the National Geographical Society, the Providence Art Club, the Handicraft Club, the Needle and Bobbin Club of New York, and the Sierra Club. She was *not* a member of the American Home Economics Association, nor was she a member of the Association of Collegiate Alumnae, both powerful lobby groups for the establishment of home economics on the Berkeley campus. Coming from the outside, without the backing of these pressure groups, she would have no easy time at Berkeley.

Not much information about Mary Patterson's first year at Berkeley exists, but a Christmas letter to President Wheeler in December 1915, one-and-one-half years after her appointment to Berkeley, indicated that her first year had been miserable. She had been close to resigning. She wrote:

> *This* Christmas is so *different* from *last* year! *Then* I was ready to *go home* and drop the whole thing. There seemed so many great obstacles to be leaped over at every turn, single-handed! You can't guess what new power and energy your friendly approval has given me. It counts a lot to us who are starting out.[44]

Wheeler knew how to reply in a fatherly manner: "What a pity I did not know that you were discouraged at the time," he responded. "I was always standing ready here to help wherever I could find a chance to help."[45]

There was no public or private word about any concrete support for building the school of home economics endorsed by the University Council and the regents. On the contrary, in the beginning of the next year, 1916, Wheeler suddenly reintroduced his idea of a department rather than a school or college for home economics.

A DEPARTMENT AFTER ALL, BUT POWER RESTS WITH THE PRESIDENT

In 1916, to the astonishment of everyone involved, President Wheeler sent a proposal to the Study-Lists Committee on Home

Economics, as the former Committee on Home Economics now called itself, requesting comments on the following propositions:

1. That a new building be provided for the work in Domestic Art and Domestic Science; and

2. That a new Department in the College of Letters and Science to be known as the Department of Home Economics be formed by uniting these subjects.[46]

The committee vehemently rejected the idea of establishing a department of home economics in the College of Letters and Science. It argued that the two subjects, domestic art and domestic science, one with a foundation in drawing and design, the other in chemistry and nutrition, are "fundamentally unrelated" and should not be united. The committee reiterated its own position that the offerings of home economics at Berkeley should aim to provide teacher training on food, clothing, and shelter; to offer graduate courses for professionals working in these areas; and to provide general academic training on the relationship of "the fundamental principles of science, economics, and art to the problems of home keeping."[47] Every course currently offered was imbedded in an already established department, that is, the course "household as an economics agent" in the department of economics, "physiology of infancy" in the department of physiology, "chemistry of textiles" in the department of chemistry. Logically, the committee argued, a department of home economics could not be established "without much overlapping or a painful process of extraction, segregation, and loss of standing."[48] It ended its letter on a note of strong discontent:

Furthermore, the Committee dares to think that through the very variety of interests represented and the impossibility of attaining thoroughness in any subject, such departments [of home economics] in other Universities will break of their own weight (or superficiality). . . . The Committee therefore, believes that the unification and consequent isolation of the courses in Domestic Art and Domestic Science which in no way claim to cover the field of Home Economics would be advantageous neither to the students, to the teaching staff, nor to the University."[49]

Wheeler overruled the committee. He had "duly considered" the committee's recommendations, but adhered, he said, to his original proposals. He confronted the committee with the news that "these proposals were accepted by the regents at their last meeting."[50] He gave the committee his instruction:

> For the purposes of administration, it is my judgment that for the coming year Miss Mary Patterson, Assistant Professor of Domestic Art, act as the Chairman of the Department. Her duties in that capacity will have to do mainly with matters connected with the budget. . . . I should like to receive the recommendation of your committee in regard to this Announcement.[51]

Wheeler had single-handedly acted against the earlier resolutions of the regents and Academic Senate. Indeed, no minutes of the regents can be found which recorded their revision of their earlier resolution in favor of the establishment of a school or college of home economics. The only related note is in the minutes of April 11, 1916, authorizing the Committee on Grounds and Buildings "to proceed with the erection of such a building for the Domestic Science Department at a cost, including equipment, not to exceed $15,000."[52] Thus the regents would have accepted Wheeler's first proposal—to erect a home economics building. There is no evidence that they approved his second proposal, the establishment of a department of home economics. As the sole communicator between the faculty and the regents, Wheeler would most certainly have been believed by the committee. No further correspondence between this committee and President Wheeler was found. The committee did not approve his proposals. It answered with silence.

In six weeks, a temporary two-story, redwood-shingled building was constructed at the northeastern corner of the campus to house the new department (see figure 7). The cost was kept within the $15,000 limit. In the fall, ninety-two women and no men enrolled in the courses offered. At the same time, the commissioner of Vocational Education of the California State Board of Education authorized the university to grant special credentials to graduates in household science, household art, and household economy.

The six-member staff of the new department was also all women: three assistant professors, one instructor in textiles, and two assistants in household art. The assistant professors were

Mary Patterson in household art and chair of the department; Agnes Fay Morgan in household science; and Josephine Davis in household science. Morgan had been moved from the Department of Nutrition in the College of Agriculture into the new department. Josephine Davis, an instructor for household science during several summer sessions at Berkeley, was made assistant professor when the department opened in the fall. No information other than their names—Ethel Taylor, Gertrude Percival, and Alice Plummer—can be found for either the instructor or the assistants.[53]

In Wheeler's eyes, the troubled matter of home economics must have finally come to a successful conclusion. He had achieved his original goal.[54] The Committee on Home Economics and the interested women had encountered a major setback, the externally strong women's lobby groups notwithstanding. They had been defeated on three levels. Their experienced and assertive appointee, Mary Kissell, had resigned after discovering that all the power was in Wheeler's hands and that all her effort was in vain due to the administration's failure to make a financial commit-

Figure 7. Home Economics Building (1916–1930) (University of California Archives)

ment. Also, the committee's rationally designed organizational structure for home economics, although approved by the regents, had been rejected in favor of the departmental structure the committee regarded as inadequate. And finally, an inexperienced individual, Mary Patterson, was now chair of the new department with little power at her disposal.

CHAPTER 3

INSTITUTION BUILDER: AGNES FAY MORGAN

A gnes Fay Morgan has related the sequence of events in 1914 that led to her appointment as an assistant professor. Dean Hunt of the College of Agriculture, who was to select her, sent his wife and teenage daughter to interview her. Considering the view of Berkeley's President Wheeler that home economics was a training for marriage and motherhood, it was, at the least, a consistent move. She passed muster, her striking red hair and diminutive stature (she was five feet two) no doubt conveying an impression of dainty femininity.

> Lucy Ward Stebbins, who was the Dean of Women here, called up one day and said she wanted to see me (she was in Chicago) and that my name had been mentioned in connection with a position to be filled on the Berkeley campus, and would I be interested? I surely would be, so I went down to her hotel and we had lunch together and a nice long visit. She decided I would be a good person for this job which was in the Department of Nutrition, then in the College of Agriculture, under the late Professor M. E. Jaffa. She came back to

Berkeley and talked to Dean Hunt, who was the Dean of the
College of Agriculture. He had his wife meet me in Chicago
the next week, and with her was her daughter, Marian, who
was then 14 years old. So evidently Mrs. Hunt also approved
of me, so I was invited to come to the University of California
as assistant professor of nutrition at 1,800 dollars a year. I
was quite pleased with this appointment.[1]

Agnes Fay Morgan may have been chosen for nonacademic reasons, but the result was a notable career of fifty years of academic
work on the Berkeley campus. Morgan shaped the department's
identity. As chair for thirty-six years, from 1918 till 1954, she tried
every conceivable means to raise the status of her department,
both by designing a curriculum consisting principally of basic science training and by conducting basic scientific research herself.
She became recognized as an outstanding scientist, but her own
prestige never elevated the status of home economics at the
University of California campus.

Born in 1884 in Peoria, Illinois, the third of four children of
Irish immigrant parents, Agnes Fay Morgan benefitted from the
accomplishments of women pioneers such as Alice Freeman
Palmer, Marion Talbot of Chicago, and Martha Carey Thomas of
Bryn Mawr, who fought for women's access to higher education and
for equal education. Her father began as a laborer after his arrival
in the United States and later became a builder.[2]

His second wife, her mother, was some sixteen years younger.
The family consisted of two boys and two girls. Neither of the boys
attended college; the girls both chose professional careers. Irene
earned a law degree from the University of Carolina and practiced
as a lawyer, and Agnes, who was offered a full college scholarship
by a local benefactor, enrolled at Vassar College and transferred to
the University of Chicago. Her B.S. degree (1904) and her M.S.
degree (1905) were in chemistry. As Rosalind Rosenberg points out
in *Beyond Separate Spheres*, the University of Chicago at the turn
of the century was a stimulating place, especially for women.[3] It
was a hotbed of feminist ideas and activities, including the
women's suffrage movement.

Although Agnes Fay had begun college with a classical liberal
arts curriculum, she found these subjects "somewhat boresome"

and turned to physics, but was still bored until she took a chemistry course taught by Julius Stieglitz at Chicago. Marion Talbot, dean of women and assistant professor of sanitary science, later professor of household administration, was teaching courses in sanitary aspects of water, food and clothing and food supplies and dietaries in the Chicago Program of Sanitary Science. Alice Norton of the Program of Home Economics and Household Arts in the College of Education taught courses on foods, chemistry of foods, household bacteriology, and the principles of cookery.[4] But Agnes Fay ignored them. The idea of taking courses in home economics, household arts, or sanitary science never crossed her mind. Her interests were the traditional nongender-based hard core sciences.

She taught chemistry for two years at Hardin-Simmons College, Montana (1905–1907) and for another year at the University of Montana (1908), where she met Arthur Ivason Morgan, a senior student in her chemistry class. She married him at the end of the year. Even by today's standards, it was unconventional for a woman teacher to date or marry one of her male students. Her marriage, like her courtship, was unusual, without the typical assumption of roles. Her husband, even though he had been her student, was four years older, having left his Oregon farm to serve in the navy in the Spanish-American War. He had been wounded and mustered out and was receiving money that made college possible for him.

After their marriage, Agnes Fay Morgan followed her husband to a teaching job in Seattle, but her own professional career was never interrupted. She taught as an instructor at the University of Washington from 1910 to 1913, concluding that a career as a chemist would require a doctorate since she "was being passed over by younger fellows who came back with Ph.D. degrees."[5] She believed, as many women scientists did at that time, that academic officials would be obliged to employ women equally if their academic qualifications and skills matched those of male colleagues.[6] Reciprocating her earlier move to Seattle, her husband followed her to the University of Chicago, where she earned a Ph.D. in organic chemistry in two years under the famous Professor Julius Stieglitz.[7] With her 1914 doctorate she joined the small group of American women who had earned such degrees. At the time only 11 percent of Ph.D.s granted were earned by women;[8] very few women earned

Ph.D.s in the sciences.[9] Even more unusual was the fact that she undertook her Ph.D. studies and obtained a faculty position as a married woman. Three of four American women who earned Ph.D.s between 1877 and 1924 were single; of the one in five college faculty in 1910 who were women, most had not married and most held the lowest ranked instructor's position.[10] On most campuses women who married were expected to resign their positions whether their husbands were employed or not.[11] Nor did single women, let alone many married women, have an equal chance at academic employment.

In the University of Illinois Archives, Margaret Rossiter found a 1914 letter from Julius Stieglitz recommending Agnes Fay Morgan for a position at the University of Illinois. In it he explained that he was recommending her because her husband was sickly. There is no note in the archives by Morgan herself referring to a job possibility at the University of Illinois.[12]

Realistic and pragmatic all her life, Morgan accepted the Berkeley offer despite the fact that it was in nutrition, that it was in the Department of Home Economics rather than the Department of Chemistry, and that male faculty at Berkeley with Ph.D.s were offered a salary, on average, of $2,400, $600 more than the amount she was offered.[13] Even an instructor without a doctorate at Berkeley could expect a salary of $1,800, the same salary to be paid to her. She may not have known of the discrepancy and probably did not know that Mary Patterson, as assistant professor in household art, who had been hired half a year before her, had no Ph.D. and yet was paid $2,000.

The Berkeley team that chose her consisted of two women, one married, one not; it probably did not matter to them whether the new faculty member was married or not, though, of course, the final decision was made by President Wheeler. President Wheeler probably agreed to hire her to satisfy some of the demands of the Committee on Home Economics and finally to go forward with establishing home economics at Berkeley.

KEEPING A "DEEP" SECRET

Morgan caught on quickly to the prevailing norms of the academic culture at Berkeley, where what was important was academic success: undertaking research, publishing in the right journals, acquiring public recognition, and attracting money for research. Family and children had no place among these criteria. The year Morgan was promoted to full professor (1923) she gave birth to her first child, a son. She was then thirty-nine, an age at which women in her generation seldom bore children. It was to be their only child.

Professor Morgan solved the problem of combining her private life as wife and mother with her public life as scientist and department chair in a simple way: she kept a significant fact of her private life a secret. Only when she was absolutely sure of her place as a full professor did she venture on motherhood, and then no one on the faculty seems to have known she was pregnant. Murdock, a former assistant to Lucy Stebbins and for many years administrative assistant in the Department of Education, wrote: "It was quite amusing: she was a chemist, rather a nutritionist, but her research was in chemistry, and so she usually wore a long smock, and when her son arrived on the scene, everybody was startled because nobody knew that he was on his way. . . . The long white apron, as it were, kept that deep secret."[14]

When Professor Morgan relayed news of the joyful event to a male colleague, he responded with coldness. "Dr. MacCollum remarked that if I had just had my fifth as he had, I'd hardly notice the event!"[15]

The birth of her son did not slow Morgan's academic productivity. She never stopped working. Her mother came to live with the new parents, and from the beginning the couple had a full-time, live-in housekeeper. Morgan put housekeeping in perspective in any case; her daughter-in-law later reported that Morgan "was not a nit-picker, a fussy housekeeper, who would constantly tell someone how to do things."[16] Their financial resources made the dual responsibilities easier to manage (see figure 8).

Agnes Fay Morgan and her husband respected each other's work. After years as headmaster of a boy's school south of San Francisco, Arthur Morgan became manager in the Sperry Flour Company and then its vice president. He never complained when she brought papers home to work on or insisted that she devote herself to him. She treated him the same. Her husband is remembered by her former students and colleagues as a kind man, with a great ability to get along with people.[17]

Figure 8. Agnes Fay Morgan, Ph.D., organic chemistry, professor of home economics 1916–1954, department chair 1918–1954 (photo 1930). (Author's private collection)

Agnes Fay Morgan believed that women were the equals of men and should be paid an equal wage, though one can only guess whether she would have considered herself a feminist.[18] Most self-described feminists of the time considered working in home economics as demeaning, an acceptance of the concept of separate "women's work," and that meant segregation and implied inferiority.[19] Of course, Morgan was not there by choice; with no offer to teach at a university in her own field, the alternative was no faculty post at all.

Morgan supported women's suffrage and endorsed and practiced birth control (many home economists did not). However, she did not join women's organizations that were critical of the societal status quo and that aimed to change society, nor was she a member of any strictly political women's organizations, such as the National Women's party, the American Women's Suffrage Association, or, later, the League of Women Voters. She kept her feminist activities within the boundaries of her profession and was an active member of twenty-one professional organizations, contributing articles to many of their newsletters. On the Berkeley campus alone, she belonged to six, mainly women's, organizations, including local chapters of national societies: the Women's Faculty Club, the Prytaneans, the Phi Beta Kappa, Omicron Nu (Honor Home Economics Society), Alpha Nu (University of California Nutrition Society), and the Berkeley chapter of the American Association of University Professors.

She was one of the initiating forces behind the creation of a national honor society for women chemists, Iota Sigma Pi, and she participated all her professional life in its national affairs. Its goals were "(1) to promote interest and enthusiasm among women students in chemistry; (2) to foster mutual advancement in academic, business and social life; (3) to stimulate personal accomplishment in chemical fields; (4) to be an example of practical efficiency among women workers."[20] Her own focus in the organization was the promotion of research; she was instrumental in establishing the society's research award and chaired its award committee for more than ten years.

In 1916 she helped to found an honor society for Berkeley women students in nutrition, Alpha Nu. Compared to Iota Sigma Pi, it had more practical goals, such as compiling syllabi of household chemistry and nutrition for high schools. Such work did not challenge women's segregated place in society, nor their low status within the university, nor did it attack any male domain. It was essentially nonconfrontational, a characteristic of most women's professional groups in the 1920s and 1930s.[21] However, the members supported each other, and they were clearly committed to excellence within their work. These groups, "compensatory recognition systems" as Rossiter has called them, provided women students and women faculty a sense of "belonging and acceptance, encouragement and psychological support, and a chance to be active in some role, including the leadership positions denied to them in male-dominated societies."[22]

Angered that *the* "Faculty" Club on the Berkeley campus allowed women faculty only the use of a corner dinner room and the so-called "powder room," where student waitresses parked their books and other paraphernalia, Morgan, together with the dean of women and other women faculty members, founded a Women's Faculty Club at Berkeley in 1919.[23] Here they could entertain visiting faculty and arrange lunch and dinner meetings.[24] The club also served as a residence for academic women, Berkeley women faculty and staff, and visitors.[25]

Morgan's educational and early professional life did not fit any particular mold. Her parents were neither highly educated, nor did they belong to the elite or upper-middle-class East Coast societies to which the parents of many of her contemporaries belonged.[26] She did not receive a degree from one of the elite eastern women's colleges, as many successful academic women of her time did. And among women who held doctorates, she was one of the few who married and had children. She may have been the only woman at the time who returned to complete a Ph.D. after she married. Even among the few women scientists she was atypical; her career was not advanced with the help of a male mentor, nor by a husband who worked in the same field and could provide her access to research facilities and money.[27] Nor did she need to retreat into more theoretical scientific fields because of a lack of access to expensive laboratory equipment.[28]

Morgan belonged to the small group of pioneer women nutritionists of the 1920s who, for the most part, were far more successful, both in rank and in salary, than their female colleagues in other fields. Strictly speaking, she was not a typical home economist either, her personal life the antithesis of all that the traditional home economics ideology embodied. She did not like to cook, nor did she keep house, nor did she care about dressing stylishly. In fact, during her first twenty years at Berkeley she was widely known for her "dowdy method of dressing," for always wearing the same shabby suit.[29] A "displaced chemist" with a superb sense of making the best out of a given situation, she seized leadership and power in the Berkeley home economics department and used her leadership position to establish status and prestige for herself in the male as well as the female spheres of academic work.

"Agnes Fay Morgan's real love, however, was administration," reads the portrait of her in *Notable American Women*,[30] and she was an effective administrator.

Organizational theory has it that a chair is crucial to the success of an academic department.[31] Cary Cherniss, in a study of the creation and history of the Department of Education and the Department of Forestry at Yale and Harvard, found "effective leadership a key element in successful creation" of an academic program.[32] He listed the following criteria for academic leadership:

> Exercising strong initiative continuously during the early years of the program's existence. . . . understanding the academic culture or an awareness that acquiring that understanding was a crucial and necessary task. . . . political finesse or organizational acumen. . . . the judicious utilization of existing and potential resources of all kinds in order to achieve the desired ends.

So, too, a leader must, perhaps paradoxically, not differ too much from those led:

> If the leader of a new program is deviant in outlook, dress, manners, or background, his program probably will be perceived as deviant also, and its chances for success will be diminished. If, on the other hand, the leader talks and dresses like the other faculty, belongs to the same clubs, has attended the same kinds of schools, and possesses the same credentials, then he, and to a great extent his program, more likely will be regarded as respectable members of the academy.[33]

The criteria cited applied to Dr. Morgan. She strongly took the initiative during her first years at Berkeley, grasped Berkeley's academic culture quickly and adapted rapidly to it, and used all possible resources toward her own goals. However, she was deviant, from both male and female faculty on campus. And she paid the price. Although she built a department that was to stand for forty-four years, from its establishment in 1918 until its end in 1962 (though it still exists subsumed in Berkeley's Department of Nutritional Sciences) what Cherniss called "deviance" in her "outlook, dress, manners, or background," and, of course, her exclusion from the "clubs" because she was a woman, kept her home economics department faculty in lesser regard than Berkeley faculty in other Berkeley schools and departments.

HOUSEHOLD "SCIENCE" OR HOUSEHOLD "ART"?

When the Department of Home Economics opened in 1916, Agnes Fay Morgan, as noted above, was moved from the division of nutrition in the College of Agriculture into the new department in the College of Letters and Science, headed by Mary Patterson, President Wheeler's appointee. This department combined the studies of household art—clothing design and construction, color theory, and interior design—with the studies of household science—nutrition, foods, and dietetics—and both fields were asked to offer courses suitable for future home economics teachers. Despite these instructions Dr. Morgan herself, in household science, taught no course designed for future home economics teachers. Instead, she offered classes in dietetics and nutrition and conducted research seminars. All of the teacher education courses were taught by Assistant Professor Josephine Davis. Dr. Morgan wrote later about her Berkeley beginnings in the College of Agriculture, and her efforts to avoid female role stereotyping:

> So I came to the University of California then, in January, 1915, and began giving courses in dietetics and nutrition, a subject I knew nothing about and nobody else knew much about at that time. I had to dig up the subject matter mostly out of German medical journals. . . . The old-fashioned cooking and arithmetic combination that had been considered to be dietetics, I would have nothing to do with. In the first place, I wasn't a very good cook and I wasn't interested in cooking.[34]

She was interested, instead, in conducting research in nutrition, especially on vitamins, and in training students in research techniques.

> I had been brought here to do something practical for the preparation of dietitians, but I wasn't able to suggest anything practical. What I wanted was to establish a scientific

foundation for the various practices that were taught as nutrition at that time.[35]

She had set up an animal research laboratory, a concentrated emphasis on research fairly unusual for any home economics program in the country at that time.

As the Committee on Home Economics had predicted, combining two unrelated subjects such as household science and household art did not work, and the awkward merger soon was sundered by competition for space and resource allocation. Neither in staff nor in content did household science and household art overlap. Household art needed space to exhibit historic costumes and design patterns and also to display art material such as weaving and tapestry received from Phoebe Hearst. Household science needed student laboratory space equipped with Bunsen burners, beakers, test tubes, and the like, and an animal research laboratory room for Dr. Morgan's colony of white rabbits. Staff from the two units literally trod on each others' toes. Lucy Stebbins, dean of women, pleaded in vain with the administration for an addition to the Department of Home Economics building.[36]

The two units of the department were incompatible in their leadership as well. Dr. Ruth Okey, a Ph.D. in organic chemistry from the University of Illinois at Urbana, who joined the faculty of household science in 1919, said of Dr. Morgan and Mary Patterson: "Miss Patterson was primarily an artist and a teacher. While she did not have the dominating personality of Dr. Morgan, the majors which she developed in Household and Decorative Art—though excellent in their field—were not very compatible with Dr. Morgan's ideas of a background in science."[37] In 1918, the Department of Home Economics recognized its two divisions and provided for a joint chairmanship and a joint budget between Patterson and Morgan, an intramural arrangement that did not work. In 1920, Morgan asked the new president, David Barrows, to establish two separate departments with separate budgets and chairs. "This is merely the formal acknowledgement of the condition which has existed since the formation of the department," she wrote. "We have at present in common no major students, no curricula, no instructors. The burden of administering the other different and uncomprehended division of the work should not be laid upon either one of us as common chairman."[38] The president acceded to her request on condition that no rearrangement of rooms or of material and equipment would be necessary.[39] There were now two women's departments in the College of Letters and Science: the Department of Household Science, headed by Agnes Fay Morgan, and the Department of Household Art, headed by Mary Patterson.[40] President Wheeler had retired in 1919, or more accurately, he had been successfully persuaded to retire, and Barrows had succeeded him.[41] With that retirement, the driving force behind a department combining household science and household art had gone.

Between 1919 and 1920, as Berkeley faculty recalled in oral history interviews, a "faculty revolution" occurred against President Wheeler's unilateral authority, with a consequent increase in faculty self-government. The faculty were especially angry that the president controlled all faculty appointments and promotions, powers that the faculty assumed upon Wheeler's departure.

The new Department of Household Science required no additional resources or administrative work. In effect, the only step that needed to be taken administratively was to initiate changes in the University's course catalog.

In addition, the transition was eased by the university's considerable confidence in Morgan's capacity for leadership, as exemplified by her efficient organization, during the war years 1917 and 1918, of a volunteer student food training program that was requested by the United States Food Administration.

GENDER INEQUALITY ENHANCED BY THE WAR

The war fostered the development of the Department of Household Science in a special way, when Ralph Merrit, former comptroller of the University of California and now federal food administrator for the State of California, recommended Morgan for the post of state secretary of volunteer college workers for California to the U.S. Federal Food Administration.[42] Dr. Morgan accepted the offer and coordinated and supervised 920 students in food conservation courses in the state's various colleges and normal schools, where teachers were trained. On the Berkeley campus, for example, the household science division offered a model series, "Emergency Courses in Food and Nutrition," intended to provide to volunteer leaders of clubs and communities information about food conservation and training in passing that information on to their communities.[43] She gave numerous public lectures urging women to conserve food and also undertook research into the nutritive value of whale and ostrich meat as possible food for human consumption. The staff of the then household science division participated in the national dietary survey carried out by Dr. Langworthy of the Home Economics Bureau of the Department of Agriculture, cooperating with the University of California Hospital in San Francisco, the University of California medical school, the Public Health Department, the Berkeley Dispensary, and the California Red Cross. A course in dietetics was designed for nurses planning to work in public health, and classes in dietetics were set up for the Red Cross.

Morgan's connections within and without the university multiplied in these years. She established a reputation as a clear, forceful speaker, an energetic organizer, and an effective administrator. The university's administration recognized her for having organized the Volunteer Student Food Training Program with only $600. When the Department of Household Science later sought collaboration for interdisciplinary research projects, specifically for setting an interdepartmental graduate group in nutrition, Morgan used her reputation and connections to advantage.

Nonetheless, there were negative consequences to the expansion of the Department of Household Sciences. The department's war offerings, which became a permanent part of the department's curricula, brought a reputation for an applied vocational orientation, with three programs: a course in dietetics for nurses; a graduate course for hospital dietitians, leading to the M.S. degree; and an extension training course for students planning to enter the fields of vocational education or rural extension organization under the provisions of the recent Smith-Lever and Smith-Hughes Acts of Congress.[44]

The negative aspect of these postwar programs was that they trained women for sterotypically female activities just as they had during the war. Even economics professor Jessica Peixotto, the first Berkeley woman faculty member, called to Washington, D.C., to head the child welfare department of the Women's Committee of the Council of National Defense, was assigned typical "women's work."[45] There, she worked closely with women such as Julia Lathrop, head of the federal Children's Bureau.

Berkeley's faculty men, in contrast, were called to head federal war service agencies; they traveled frequently to Washington as consultants to special war committees or spent a year abroad in charge of governmental agencies, such as the American Expeditionary Forces in France and the American Red Cross. John Merriam, a professor of paleontology and historical geology, served as director of the National Research Council, which, through its connection with the National Council of Defense "proved to be the most important wartime scientific body in America."[46]

Berkeley women could not fail to be aware of the fact that their services were recognized as less academically stimulating and that they led to fewer powerful political alliances than the war activities of most of the male faculty. Lucy Stebbins, the dean of women, expressed this sense in her 1917 through 1918 annual report to the president:

It is not easy to feel the joy of sacrifice and service in pursuing the humdrum routine of education while men are called out to practice new arts, to manage machines more powerful and complex than the world has ever seen and to give their lives for their country. But the women of the University have been faithful to the task imposed upon them.[47]

The new curricular offerings allowed the Department of Home Economics to hire more faculty—Anna Williams, Alice Metcalf, and Elizabeth Bridge—and thus enlarged the department to a "critical mass" of people. Yet the department's campus reputation became one of applied and vocational studies, both regarded as below Berkeley's standards. The department had no choice in the matter. With Berkeley a public university, the state Department of Education had both the right and the budgetary power to force Berkeley's Department of Home Economics to respond to its requirements.

BUILDING AN INSTITUTION: A GENIUS FOR ESSENTIALS

"Female institution building," an expression coined by Estelle Freedman, professor of history at Stanford, describes the separatist political strategy of creating a public female sphere with the purpose of achieving an egalitarian future.[48] Freedman argued that female political leaders who had power over their own jurisdiction (women), would gain leverage also in the political arena at large.[49] At certain times and in certain societies, the creation of a public female sphere might indeed have been the only viable political strategy for women.

Agnes Fay Morgan, like other pioneering home economists in the 1920s, was a true institution builder. She created a place where women scientists and students could undertake academic work, constantly urging them to earn academic respectability and to undertake research. She created research opportunities, especially for her doctoral students, helping to forge bonds between her doctoral students and women chemists through the Iota Sigma Pi. She placed a number of doctoral students in faculty positions at other universities. Still, the supportive dominion for her women students was not a nurturing place for her faculty, particularly those who were not her former students. In a position that required force and skill, she centralized power in her department, reinforcing the distance between herself and the rest of the faculty.[50] She centralized material resources for research, too, and gathered around her the best graduate students. Ruth Okey, her colleague for thirty-four years, said such autocratic traits discouraged the staff:

> She was always right. Some of her staff learned to suggest a change indirectly in such a way that Dr. Morgan was convinced that the idea was her own, otherwise her response was likely to be, "Nonsense!" This characteristic was responsible for the brief stays of several very able staff appointees.[51]

To some this pattern seemed a consequence of gender. When the dean of the College of Agriculture, Claude Hutchison, who served from 1931 to 1952, was asked what he would do if he had a chance to do things over again—in 1938 the department was moved into the College of Agriculture and reported to the dean of agriculture—he responded, "I think I would bring some men into the field. . . . I don't know why it is you girls, you women never like to work for women as well as you like to work for men."[52]

However autocratic and driven Morgan may have appeared in her professional sphere, however, she had the power to forget her battles at work and relax with Agatha Christie novels and a glass of scotch when she was at home.[53]

Morgan did use all the authority and power available to the chair of a department, and in a department of all women she had more authority than she would have had elsewhere. In a male department, she hardly could have managed to become chair or stay chair for such a long time. She would not have had access to resources and the know-how to get them. She would not have traveled to as many conferences or served on as many campus and national committees if she had needed to ask someone's permission for her absence and the use of travel funds. No building would have been named after her, as one was in 1961. Freedman maintains that the leverage of a separate women's sphere should lead to "political leverage in larger society." This leverage did exist for Morgan; it did not for the members of her department.

Although Morgan tried, whenever possible, to break out of the separate sphere of women's work, she never suggested a merger with any other department, only a name change. Perhaps she thought nothing else was possible. Perhaps she realized that her own personal success depended on the existence of a separate sphere. In any case, she turned the discrimination demonstrated by male faculty and male professional associations into positive results. She gained power, status, and prestige within her own ranks. She helped other women scientists elsewhere even though at Berkeley only her own doctoral students benefitted.

During the early years of the program's existence, Morgan broke up the forced unity of household art and household science. She understood the academic culture and contested the preeminence of vocational courses introduced in response to the demands of war. In the university eulogy at the time of her death, she was remembered by her staff for her organizational skill and political finesse, and for distinguishing the essential from the trivial. "She had a sublime confidence in her rightness and a genius for disregarding nonessentials and relaxing when the opportunity presented itself."[54]

CHAPTER 4

IN SEARCH OF STATUS

Margaret Rossiter, in her book *Women Scientists in America, Struggles and Strategies to 1940*, wrote that "Treading the narrow path between the two cultures [female and academic culture] and meeting the pressure for both prestige and practicality would be a continuing and dominant theme throughout the history of home economics."[1]

Home economics programs around the country, such as those at the University of Chicago, University of Wisconsin, Pennsylvania State University, Columbia University Teachers College, faced the same narrow path as that at Berkeley. They had to be responsive to their state legislatures' demands for practical education and simultaneously adhere to the scientific standards of the academic community at their campuses. They were unable to avoid a reputation as trade school departments that lowered their status on campus. Hoping to increase the academic respectability of the program, in response to the demand from the academic community to adhere to scientific standards, they overloaded the curriculum with science requirements, and they hired mainly women doctorates.[2] The Berkeley department, under the tight control of Agnes Fay Morgan, was linked to other "more respectable" departments, such as biochemistry and physiology, through an interdepartmental graduate group in nutrition (Professor Morgan became its director in 1946). Morgan sought visibility for the department and herself by active participation in the campus administration. She also sought, and received, a larger and more prominent space than the temporary war building that housed the household science department from 1916 to 1930. She and the other members of the department took part in many national and international conferences that brought attention to the department outside California and a good reputation for it in the profession. As chair, Morgan developed ties to state agriculture and food industry groups and lobbied them for financial support during the days of limited resource allocation. She tried several times to change the department's name to human nutrition, both to reflect more properly the work it did and to rid the department of an image invariably associated with vocational work of low academic quality—that prepared women "with rule-of-thumb recipes for gracious living."[3]

Martin Trow, in "Analysis of Status,"[4] analyzes the factors that affect high or low prestige and status in academic systems and lists as primary ones the quality of the faculty, students, and academic curriculum; the faculty's research productivity, research awards, and success in attracting outside research funds; the prestige of graduates' career choices and employment; space and research facilities; faculty service on important campus committees; and support from the administration and related departments. At research universities, the aggregate research reputation contributes most importantly to a department's prestige. The factors Trow names are also the criteria used for assessing the ranking of American universities. Trow pointed out that in academic systems status plays an unusually strong role, replacing money as the primary coin of exchange. Dr. Morgan's efforts on behalf of the household science department did fulfill many of these conditions, yet during her tenure the department was low in prestige, status, and power.

CONCENTRATING ON WHAT AFFECTS STATUS: QUALITY OF FACULTY, CURRICULUM, RESEARCH, OUTSIDE FUNDING, GRADUATES' CAREERS, COMMITTEE SERVICE, AND FACILITIES

In 1918, when household science became a separate division within the Department of Home Economics, its faculty consisted of five members: two assistant professors, Dr. Morgan and Josephine Davis (Wharton); one instructor, Anna Williams; and two assistants, Alice Metcalf and Elizabeth Bridge. Of these, only Agnes Fay Morgan held a Ph.D. This situation changed drastically once the department became independent. Four of the faculty were hired as assistant professors. Of the thirteen members employed in household science between 1920 and 1938, eleven held Ph.D.s from universities such as Berkeley, Chicago, Columbia, Cornell, Illinois, Iowa, Yale, and Washington (see table 4.1). Even the four instructors (three later became assistant professors) had doctorates. Only the two assistants, who stayed for less than two years, did not. Icie Gertrude Macy (Hoobler), one instructor, was a Yale graduate, with a B.S. from the University of Chicago in chemistry in 1916 with the same Julius Stieglitz under whom Agnes Fay Morgan had written her dissertation. When her interests shifted from inorganic chemistry to physiological chemistry and nutrition—a field more open to women—Macy entered the Sheffield Scientific School at Yale University to study for her doctorate under Lafayette B. Mendel, one of the few early male mentors for women in this field. Dr. Macy, who became a pioneer in many professional roles for women and a nationally and internationally known nutritionist, left Berkeley in 1928 to head the nutrition research project at the Merrill-Palmer School of Detroit. In 1928, she was a charter member of the American Institute of Nutrition, and in 1930 and 1931 became the first woman to chair a division of the American Chemical Society. For twenty-five years she directed nutrition research at the Children's Fund of Michigan.[5]

This impressive number of doctorates among the department staff at a time when it was still common at the university to become a faculty member without a Ph.D. reflected Morgan's understanding of the importance of the quality of the faculty to a department.[6] However, the household art department did not hire a Ph.D. until 1932, with the appointment of Lila Morris O'Neale, a Berkeley graduate in anthropology (see table 4.1). Morgan's failure to support and encourage her junior staff undermined her department's standing when her decisive leadership style and the pressure from the administration coupled with the limited university budget of the Depression years led to high staff turnover between 1920 and 1938.[7]

Table 4.1: Home Economics Staff 1916–1935

1916/17	1918/19	1920/21
Home Economics	Home Economics	Home Economics
	Div. Household Science	*Dept. Household Science*
Mary F. Patterson Assistant Prof. of Household Art	Agnes F. Morgan, Ph.D. Assistant Prof. of Household Science	Agnes F. Morgan, Ph.D. Associate Prof. of Household Science
Agnes F. Morgan, Ph.D. Assistant Prof. of Household Science	Josephine D. Wharton, M.A. Assistant Prof. of Household Science	Ruth Okey, Ph.D. Assistant Prof. of Household Science
Josephine E. Davis, M.A. Assistant Prof. of Household Science	Anna Waller Williams, M.A. Instructor in Household Science	Icie Macy, Ph.D. Instructor in Household Science
Ethel E. Taylor, B.S. Instructor in Textiles	Alice Metcalf, A.B. Assistant in Household Science	Anita Lassen, A.B. Assistant in Household Science
Gertrude Percival, A.B. Laboratory Assistant in Household Art	Elizabeth Bridge, M.A. Assistant in Household Science	
Alice G. Plummer, M.A. Assistant in Household Art	*Div. Household Art*	*Dept. Household Art*
	Mary F. Patterson Assistant Prof. of Household Art	Mary F. Patterson Associate Prof. of Household Art
	Ethel E. Taylor, B.S. Instructor in Textiles	Anne Swainson, M.A. Associate in Textiles
	Helen Fancher Instructor in Household Art	Helen Fancher Associate in Household Art
	Eveline P. Cutler Director of Red Cross Work	Mae Lent Associate in Household Art
	John W. Gilmore, M.S. Professor of Agronomy*	John W. Gilmore, M.S. Professor of Agronomy*

*Professor John Gilmore did not appear anywhere in any fields, nor was he listed as having taught any courses.

Source: University of California Catalogs, U.C. Archives, Bancroft Library.

Table 4.1: Home Economics Staff 1916–1935 (cont'd.)

1925/26	1930/31	1935/36
Home Economics	Home Economics	Home Economics
Dept. Household Science	*Dept. Household Science*	*Dept. Household Science*
Agnes F. Morgan, Ph.D. Professor of Household Science	Agnes F. Morgan, Ph.D. Professor of Household Science	Agnes F. Morgan, Ph.D. Professor (Chair) of Household Science
Ruth Okey, Ph.D. Assistant Prof. of Household Science	Ruth Okey, Ph.D. Associate Prof. of Household Science	Ruth Okey, Ph.D. Associate Prof. of Household Science
Lucille Johnson, Ph.D. Instructor in Household Science	Florence A. Armstrong, Ph.D. Assistant Prof. of Household Science	Helen Gillum, Ph.D. Instructor in Household Science
		Irene Sanborn Hall, Ph.D. Instructor in Household Science
Dept. Household Art	*Dept. Household Art*	*Dept. Household Art*
Mary F. Patterson Associate Prof. of Household Art & Design	Mary F. Patterson Associate Prof. of Household Art & Design	Mary F. Patterson Associate Prof. (Chair) of Household Art & Design
Hope Gladding Assistant Prof. of Household Art & Design	Hope Gladding Associate Prof. of Household Art & Design	Hope Gladding Associate Prof. of Household Art & Design
Helen Fancher Associate in Household Art	Helen Fancher Associate in Household Art	Lila M. O'Neale, Ph.D. Associate Prof. of Household Art
Mae Lent Associate in Household Art	Mae Lent Associate in Household Art	Helen Fancher Associate in Household Art
		Mae Lent Associate in Household Art

Besides Morgan and Okey, only three of the twelve women employed in the Department of Household Science during this time stayed longer than four years. Lucille Johnson, a Ph.D. from Columbia, was instructor from 1923 until 1926 and assistant professor from 1926 to 1928. Helen Gillum, with a master's from Teachers' College in Columbia and a Ph.D. in nutrition from Berkeley, worked for one year as an instructor after completion of her doctorate in 1935 and joined the tenured faculty rank in 1936 (see figure 9). She remained in the department as a full professor until her retirement in 1958. Betty Monaghan Watts, a Ph.D. from the University of Washington, joined the department in 1936 as an instructor and was an assistant professor from 1941 to 1944. The academic staff of the department steadily expanded from four pro-

Figure 9. Helen Gillum, assistant professor of household science (photo 1936) (University of California Archives)

fessors in 1940 to eight professors in 1954, with another eleven Ph.D.s joining the department in those years (see table 4.2).

From the very beginning of her appointment at Berkeley, Professor Morgan pursued another strategy: building an extremely "scientific" curriculum based on fundamental principles of science. She ran into a structural bind. Since Berkeley was a land-grant university, it was required to comply with a California State Department of Education request that the department train high school teachers and other service professionals to work as dietetics and agriculture extension consultants. Dr. Okey recalled:

In the early years in Letters and Science, she [Morgan] had to deal on the one hand with university administrators, such as President Benjamin Ide Wheeler, who were strongly oriented toward high academic standards and had little respect for home economics, and, on the other hand, with a state Department of Education which demanded teachers trained in the practical aspects of home cooking and sewing, and dietitians who could deal with problems of quantity cookery and food management as well as therapeutic dietetics.[8]

Dr. Morgan would not compromise on the scientific foundation for all work in nutrition despite these pressures. The curriculum developed by the Berkeley department she regarded with pride as "the only one in the country that has stuck by that." Most home economics departments in her opinion "did not demand very much in the way of scientific basis. We demand general chemistry, organic chemistry, biochemistry, physiology, bacteriology, and quantitative analysis, and of course, statistics. That's the minimum that's required of the undergraduate."[9]

Keeping the home economics curriculum on a strong scientific base became a permanent struggle throughout her thirty-six years as chair of the department. She recalled:

But all aspects of [home economics] do not lend themselves to that treatment, and I found it increasingly difficult to maintain a high type of scholarship with solid research background for all parts of this department that the teacher trainers wanted us to maintain.[10]

Table 4.2: Home Economics Staff 1940–1964

1940/41	1945/46	1950/51
Agnes F. Morgan, Ph.D. Prof., Home Econ., Chair	Agnes F. Morgan, Ph.D. Prof., Home Econ., Chair	Agnes F. Morgan, Ph.D. Prof., Home Econ., Chair
Ruth Okey, Ph.D. Assoc. Prof., Home Econ.	Ruth Okey, Ph.D. Prof., Home Econ.	Ruth Okey, Ph.D. Prof., Home Econ.
Helen L. Gillum, Ph.D. Asst. Prof., Home Econ.	Helen L. Gillum, Ph.D. Assoc. Prof., Home Econ.	Helen L. Gillum, Ph.D. Assoc. Prof., Home Econ.
Catherine Landreth, Ph.D. Asst. Prof., Home Econ.	Catherine Landreth, Ph.D. Assoc. Prof., Home Econ.	Catherine Landreth, Ph.D. Assoc. Prof., Home Econ. Lect., Psychology
Martha J. Kremer, Ph.D. Instr., Home Econ.	Jessie Coles, Ph.D. Assoc. Prof., Home Econ.	Jessie Coles, Ph.D. Prof., Home Econ.
Betty Watts, Ph.D. Instr., Home Econ.	Bessie B. Cook, Ph.D. Asst. Prof., Home Econ.	Bessie B. Cook, Ph.D. Asst. Prof., Home Econ.
Mae Lent Assoc., Home Econ.	Barbara Kennedy, Ph.D. Instr., Home Econ.	Barbara Kennedy, Ph.D. Asst. Prof., Home Econ.
Ellen B. McGowan, Ph.D. Lect., Textiles	Agnes C. McClelland, M.A. Assoc., Home Econ.	Judson Landis, Ph.D. Assoc. Prof., Home Econ.
	Jean Warrren, Ph.D. Asst. Prof., at Davis	M. Virginia Jones, Ph.D. Asst. Prof., Textiles
	Winifred C. Irwin, M.A. Instr., at Davis	Lotte Arnrich, B.S. Lect., Home Econ.
	Hazel V. Schulze, Ph.D. Instr., at Davis	Margaret Bremner Hanson, M.S. Lect., Home Econ.
		Agnes C. McClelland, M.A. Assoc., Home Econ.
		Eve W. Straight, B.S. Lect., Institution Management
		Barbara I. Keane, M.S. Lect., Home Econ.

Sources: General Catalogs 1940–1964; Faculty Bibliographies, U.C. Archives, Bancroft Library, Berkeley.

Table 4.2: Home Economics Staff 1940–1964 (cont'd)

1954/56	1960/61	1964/65
Agnes F. Morgan, Ph.D. Prof. Emeritus, Home Econ.	George M. Briggs, Ph.D. Prof., Nutrition, Chair	George M. Briggs, Ph.D. Prof., Nutrition, Chair
Ruth Okey, Ph.D. Prof., Home Econ.	Ruth Okey, Ph.D. Prof., Nutrition	Doris H. Calloway, Ph.D. Prof., Nutrition
Helen L. Gillum, Ph.D. Assoc. Prof., Home Econ.	Mary Ann Morris. Ph.D. Assoc. Prof., Nutrition	Maynard A. Joslyn, Ph.D. Prof., Food Technology
Catherine Landreth, Ph.D. Assoc. Prof., Home Econ. Lect., Psychology	Catherine Landreth, Ph.D. Prof., Home Econ. Lect., Psychology	Gordon Mackinney, Ph.D. Prof., Food Technology
Jessie Coles, Ph.D. Prof., Home Econ., Chair	Jessie Coles, Ph.D. Prof., Home Econ.	Sheldon Margen, M.D. Prof., Human Nutrition and Social Welfare
Bessie B. Cook, Ph.D. Assoc. Prof., Home Econ.	Bessie B. Cook, Ph.D. Assoc. Prof., Nutrition	Harold S. Olcott, Ph.D. Prof., Marine Food Sci.
Barbara Kennedy, Ph.D. Asst. Prof., Home Econ.	Barbara Kennedy, Ph.D. Asst. Prof., Nutrition	Barbara M. Kennedy, Ph.D. Asst. Prof., Nutrition
Judson Landis, Ph.D. Assoc. Prof., Family Sociology	Judson Landis, Ph.D. Prof., Family Sociology	Judson Landis, Ph.D. Prof., Family Sociology
M. Virginia Jones, Ph.D. Asst. Prof., Textiles	Richard L. Lyman, Ph.D. Asst. Prof., Nutrition	Richard L. Lyman, Ph.D. Assoc. Prof., Nutrition
Lotte Arnrich, Ph.D. Instr., Home Econ.	Mary Ann Williams, Ph.D. Asst. Prof., Nutrition	Mary Ann Williams, Ph.D. Assoc. Prof., Nutrition
Margaret B. Hanson, M.S. Assoc., Home Mgmnt. Supvr., Teaching of Home Econ.	Kaye Funk, M.S. Assoc. Institution Mgmnt.	Robert Stockstad, Ph.D. Prof., Nutrition
Agnes C. McClelland, M.A. Assoc., Home Econ.	Agnes C. McClelland, M.A. Lect., Home Econ.	W. Duane Brown, Ph.D. Assoc. Prof., Marine Food Sci.
Clark E. Vincent, Ph.D. Instr., Family Sociology	Rosemarie Ostwald, Ph.D. Assoc., Nutrition	Rosemarie Ostwald, Ph.D. Asst. Prof., Nutrition
Barbara I. Keane, M.S. Lect., Home Econ.	Hannah Sanders, M.A. Assoc., Home Econ.	Mildred J. Bennett, Ph.D. Lect., Nutrition
Valerie Smola, M.A. Assoc., Home Management	Willa H. Schmidt, M.S. Assoc., Home Mgmnt.	Ellsworth Dougherty, Ph.D., M.D. Lect., Comp. Nutrition
Winifred Wilkinson, B.S. Assoc., Institution Admin.	Henrietta Henderson, B.S. Certified Dietitian Lect., Hospital Dietetics	Henrietta Henderson, B.S. Certified Dietitian Lect., Hospital Dietetics
Dorothy M. Sidwell, M.S. Assoc., Home Econ.	Ruth L. Hueneman, D.Sc. Assoc. Prof., Public Health and Nutrition	Karl Folkers, Ph.D. Lect., Vitamin Chem.
Ruth L. Hueneman, D.Sc. Lect., Home Econ.	Helen V. Park Lect., Home Econ.	Cecil Entenman, Ph.D. Lect., Nutri. Sci.
Evelyn Peters, M.A. Lect., Home Econ.		Ruth L. Hueneman, D.Sc. Assoc. Prof., Public Health
		Samuel Lepkovsky, Ph.D. Prof., Poultry Husbandry
		Virginia R. McMasters, M.S. Lect., Dietetics
		Ruth Steinkamp, M.D. Lec., Human Nutrition

Morgan also became known for her high standards outside her own Berkeley department. In many articles she pleaded for a science-based curriculum; she scolded other home economics departments: "The 'pure' sciences have so hastily become applied sciences that little but the applications seem to have survived."[11] She sharply dismissed all "watered-down" home economics curriculums—the cooking, table setting, and routine calculations were in her opinion "wholly unnecessary except as they offer illustration of principles or even comic relief. Students can be interested in both scientific and social concepts through the vital avenue of human nurture, often spelled nutrition."[12]

A *Journal of Home Economics* article by Morgan described a professional home economics curriculum of three components: at least 60 percent should be devoted to the foundation disciplines, 10 percent to the home economics core, and the remaining 30 percent to general education.[13] Her efforts to establish a scholarly curriculum are lauded in every subsequent commemorative article about her life.[14]

Morgan chose a program of academic rigor, as others did in similar situations, by requiring that home economics students take additional courses to increase their academic respectability. Candidates for teaching credentials thus found themselves prepared to teach (and often did teach) basic science courses in high school, rather than the traditional cooking and sewing.[15]

Students training to be teachers nevertheless complained, and the administration criticized the department for overly rigorous requirements. Monroe Deutsch, dean of the university, and, later, provost of the faculty from 1930 to 1947, wrote to Dr. Morgan in such a vein:

Some time ago my attention was called to certain aspects of your course Household Science 120. I am informed that the course itself is felt to be of great value to those taking it, it is included as one of the absolute requirements for the major in Household Science. In addition to the regular work in the course (lectures and laboratory work which always take more time than the amount supposedly required), I have been informed that an additional rat problem [undertaking a research problem which required work on rats] is demanded of the students; indeed two such problems were demanded.

This is, I am informed, beside the regular laboratory work. I am informed that during the course of the semester this problem will probably take 150 hours beside the amount which the students have a right to expect. . . . There is a limit to what a student can do. . . . I think the matter should be given careful consideration by you and your colleagues.[16]

At the fortieth reunion of the class of 1947, former home economics students, asked about their extracurricular life on campus, unanimously replied that they had no time for any activities other than attending classes and feeding rats![17]

Such heavy emphasis on fundamental science ought to have brought the department high recognition from the university administration and acceptance by related disciplines and departments. But it did not. In view of the service orientation and the emphasis on teacher training mandated by the state, the academic community at Berkeley still considered the department a "trade school department." Home economics constantly had to seek to legitimize and defend its academic standards.

Even the many research projects undertaken by the members of the department did little to diminish the trade school image. In the eyes of the rest of the campus, the department's research was applied research, that is, it did not extend into frontiers of pure science, "pure in the sense of lacking immediate applicability to already recognized problems."[18] Its work, rather, was concerned with the practical needs of women, children, and family, and not such research topics as brought academic status and prestige.

In the twenty-first Lenna Frances Cooper Memorial Lecture at the annual meeting of the American Dietetic Association in Anaheim in 1983, the professor and provost of nutritional science, Doris Calloway, in an analysis of historical and contemporary research contributions by women and men in the field of nutrition, found a gender difference between researchers' concerns: "Men explore problems; women study needs."[19] "Women were the principal investigators of the nutritional concerns of women and children, for reasons of access and gentility."[20] Women in nutrition, Calloway argued, entered the field with a Ph.D. in chemistry, but found employment in departments of home economics. They fostered their research through cooperation with the agricultural experiment stations. Few had the opportunity to conduct "pure" research, in view of narrow departmental boundaries. Their most readily available subjects for study were women, and the resources available to them, such as the Purnell Funds, were earmarked for studies to improve the condition of women, children, and the home. However, men in nutrition, while they also usually entered the field from chemistry, found employment in chemistry or related fields such as physiological chemistry, biochemistry, physiology, and sometimes medicine. Their research interests tended to be related to farm animals, or, if to human beings, to principally clinical problems, such as hazards of obesity or anatomical defects caused by rickets and similar diseases.[21] The topics men chose to study generally enjoyed high status. Such a gender-dictated choice of research topics was prevalent at Berkeley, as elsewhere.

Dr. Morgan's own first research projects were a consequence of a need to find something to teach. She was brought to Berkeley "to do something practical for the preparation of dietitians," but with few books available on nutrition, she set up her first vitamin research projects and used her results as teaching materials.[22] These early projects dealt with the nutrients of food produced in California and with the effects of processing on food values. She was concerned with heat treatment's impact on the nutritional efficiency of proteins in wheat, almonds, walnuts, and pressure-cooked meat,[23] a practical household problem. Men in nutrition, at that time, Professor Jaffa for example, concentrated on animal feeds and commercial products.

During her career Dr. Morgan undertook research in three main areas: human nutrition, animal nutrition, and food technology, with the results of her work published in professional journals such as *The American Journal of Diseases of Children.* In human nutrition she was the first to observe the effect of a commonly used food preservative, sulfur dioxide, on vitamin content, finding that sulfur dioxide had a protective effect on vitamin C and a damaging effect on thiamine. She also studied the causes of low weight in children, with research on the effect of small supplementary feedings such as fruits, milk, and wheat germ on the growth of school children. She undertook research in animal nutrition also, because animals can be more readily controlled under laboratory conditions than human subjects can and findings can be applied to the improvement of human nutrition. Using various animals—rats and, later, guinea pigs, hamsters, and cocker spaniels—she analyzed the relationships between vitamins and hormone activities. Her work on dietary calcium and phosphorus, vitamin D, and the parathyroid gland demonstrated the danger of giving babies excessive amounts of vitamin D.

Many of Dr. Morgan's findings were unnoticed by the medical profession, despite a report in a scientific journal on nutrition, only to be rediscovered years later. Her most "basic" research brought her the most recognition, although ten years after her findings were published. In 1939, she discovered that pantothenic acid, a B vitamin, is essential for adrenal function and for normal pigmentation of hair and skin. She had found that the fur of black rats began to turn gray from adrenal damage when their diet lacked the vitamin B complex. Not until 1949 was she acknowledged for such basic research when she received the prestigious Garvan Medal of the American Chemical Society (see figure 10), and in 1954, the year of her retirement at age seventy, the Borden Award from the American Institute of Nutrition. Earlier national recognition certainly would have eased much of her struggle on her home campus. Rossiter has noted that "these early women winners were highly deserving of their awards, but should have received them years earlier."[24]

Since the graying pattern of the rats resembled the markings of the fashionable silver fox furs, Morgan, always practical, persuaded a commercial breeder of fur foxes to feed a few of his young foxes a pantothenate-low diet. They showed pattern graying, and whenever she gave a talk on her work on pantothenic acid deficiency Morgan proudly wore a stunning fur stole: two pelts sewed together made from the fur of sibling foxes. One pelt came from the experimental control fox, fed pantothenic acid concentrate. It had a deep and lustrous shiny black coat with long gray hair.[25] The other pelt came from the deficiently fed fox. It was one-half the size of the other and a dingy gray. She wore the stole in 1939 at the annual meeting of the American Society for Experimental Biology and also during her acceptance speech for the Garvan Award in 1949, to the delight of the participants (see figure 11). Ruth Okey recollected that "the long guard hairs were missing in the fur of the deficient fox and that the scarf soon began to look 'moth-eaten.' "[26]

Before Morgan's retirement she had published around 200 papers, a textbook (*Experimental Food Study*), with colleague and friend Irene Sanborn Hall, and 77 review articles. After her retirement she wrote some 40 more papers. She summarized the results of a study of the nutritional status of older people in California, a longitudinal study begun in 1938, and in the publication *Nutritional Status USA* reviewed and collated 179 publications on this subject by U.S. Experiment Stations (see figure 12).

As prolific a researcher and writer as Dr. Morgan was, she was not the only one in her department. Ruth Okey and Helen Gillum and a number of their graduate students published results of their research in journals such as the *Journal of the American Chemical Society*, the *American Journal of Physiology*, the *Journal of Biological Chemistry*, and the *Journal of Nutrition*. Okey studied the monthly changes in the metabolism of women during their

Figure 10. A. F. Morgan with Garvan Medal (1949) (Author's private collection)

Figure 11. A.F. Morgan wearing the results of the award-winning research, the normal and the pantothenic acid-deficient fox furs (October 1941) (Author's private collection)

menstrual cycles to determine the basal metabolic rate and to analyze blood and urine (see figure 13). Graduate students in the department and women students from physical education served as research subjects and assistants. In a 1981 essay about her experience as a women scientist at Berkeley, Okey recalled that this research project was described in the *San Francisco Chronicle* by a "facetious editor" under the title "A Tablespoon of Blood for Your Breakfast."[27] She continued to study lipid metabolism using rats and other laboratory animals until her retirement in 1961; fifty or so publications resulted from this research, leading, in turn, to research on cholesterol and lecithin. Okey made *cholesterol* a notorious word in Berkeley long before it became known worldwide.[28]

During the Depression Okey sought to find "an adequate diet at low cost."[29] She participated in the Heller Committee of the University of California, which priced budgets for families at vari-

Figure 12. Agnes Fay Morgan: Awards and publications (photo 1962) (Author's private collection)

ous income levels and analyzed the nutritive value of diets at various costs for the state of California. In 1941, together with the respected Berkeley professor of social economics, Emily Huntington, she was appointed to serve on President Roosevelt's First Nutrition Congress. She had more than 100 publications and various reviews. Even so, Okey never gained as much recognition as did Dr. Morgan. One may speculate that she was less renowned because her research topics were even more related to women than those of Agnes Fay Morgan, or there may have been other factors such as a personality less forceful than the department chair's and the sparseness of research facilities and research funding within the department. Dr. Morgan, as chair of the department, had first

Figure 13. Ruth Okey, Ph.D. organic chemistry, professor of home economics 1919–1960, department chair 1955–1960 (photo circa 1917) (Author's private collection)

choice in allocation of the limited resource funds, and she used this power to advantage.

Despite limited resources, the department as a whole produced respectable results. In 1933 alone, the four members of the staff published thirteen scientific articles. Dr. Morgan's motto that "in every home economics division of colleges and universities an active effective research program shall dominate" was upheld within her own department.

SECURING OUTSIDE RESEARCH FUNDING

Another factor determining the prestige of an academic department is its ability to attract inside or outside funding for research. In this respect the Department of Home Economics was only partially successful. Professor Morgan, in her closing remarks at the symposium in 1965 honoring her anniversary at Berkeley, told the audience, "My first troubles were budgetary. A tight-fisted board of research gave us $600 one year for the research of the department and I considered this a remarkable windfall. However, I found later that they had given the Chemistry Department $13,000 for their research. This I considered obviously unfair. I think no one would agree with me then or now."[30]

Unable to secure funding from campus sources, the department tried outside sources, such as California's agriculture and food industry, and garnered support for work in analyzing vitamin A content in citrus fruit juices; vitamin A and B changes in artichokes during canning and in tomatoes during ripening (important for knowing when to harvest); and possible ways to enrich flour with vitamins. The faculty-administration Board of Research at Berkeley complained that problems of interest to the food industry did not require *real* research. In 1934 board Chairman Armin Leuschner wrote to the provost.

> After careful consideration of the propriety of the tests on bread and milk for the National Oil Products Company and the proposed tests on milk for the Arden Gold Seal Farms, Inc., we recommend that the new tests be undertaken for a limited time only, to give Mrs. Morgan an opportunity "to

make a comparison as to biological value and constancy of vitamin content" of the products of the two companies, and that
the milk and bread tests for both the National Oil Products
Company and the Arden Seal Farms, Inc., be discontinued on
June 30, 1935. . . .

We are appreciative of the fact that her departmental and
research budgets have been severely cut and that these tests
furnish funds and at the same time give employment to young
women who have been trained in the University. These reasons, however, do not appear to us to be sufficient to answer
the criticisms which we would invite by continuing such tests
except in cases involving real research projects.[31]

Many of the Berkeley administrators considered this tainted
research, "not only for its service orientation but also for its seem-
ing triviality."[32]

Starting in 1938 when the dean of the College of Agriculture,
Claude Hutchison, instigated the move of home economics from the
College of Letters and Science to the College of Agriculture, the
department gained access to more research money through the
Agricultural Experiment Station. These added funds, Okey said,
"helped only the chair."[33] Okey had to stop her own research on
guinea pigs due to a lack of funds.

Given the limited funds the department did receive both from
within and without the university, it is amazing that it undertook
as many research projects as it did. But funded or not, little of this
work translated into status for the department.

The Career Choices and Employment of the Department's Students and the Graduate Group in Nutrition

Department members realized that, of all factors affecting status, a
Ph.D. program carried the most weight academically. It became Dr.
Morgan's aim to lead her students to a successful completion of a
Ph.D. in nutrition. She eventually succeeded.

The first household science student, Statie Erikson, who
applied for admission to candidacy for the Ph.D. in nutrition in
1924 had to meet with a special Provisional Subcommittee to test

her fitness for such candidacy. Miss Erikson had already fulfilled all stated requirements, but Dean Charles Lipman of the Graduate Division was convinced nonetheless that

> there seems to be a lack of fundamental training, perhaps in chemistry, and a lack of the original attitude toward scientific problems in the case of Miss Erikson which makes this special procedure with regard to her admission to candidacy necessary. . . . While we recognize the extra amount of work involved in such task, we feel that we are doing it in the interests of the standards of the university.[34]

On this subcommittee were Professors Morgan and Okey from the Department of Household Science, Burnett from the Department of Physiology, Porter from the Department of Chemistry, and Schmidt and Sundstroem from the Department of Biochemistry. The biochemistry faculty questioned "whether or not the thesis problem was a sufficiently definite one that positive results could be assured with another year's work." Professor Burnett left the meeting before it finished, and the votes of Porter, Morgan, and Okey, in favor of Erickson's candidacy, were insufficient.[35] Erikson was asked to return in six months with a more definite outline for her thesis. Dr. Morgan protested the outcome in a letter to Dean Lipman:

> I believe that a serious injustice is being done the candidate by the discouraging and unnecessary delay here brought about, and I must confess that Miss Okey and I are both alarmed and incensed by the attitude of certain of our colleagues toward our research program.[36]

Indeed discouraged, Erikson left Berkeley to join the faculty of the University of Kentucky. In 1930, she completed her dissertation and successfully passed her orals. She later became professor and dean of home economics.

Once Morgan realized that she would not succeed in turning her department into a department of nutrition, she helped set up an interdepartmental graduate group in nutrition, combining the fields of biochemistry, physiology, anatomy, medicine, and household science. This group, chaired by Carl L. Schmidt, professor of biochemistry, from 1930 until 1946, was in the early days officially called "Animal Nutrition," reflecting the research emphasis of the male faculty in the field.

During the Schmidt tenure as chair, home economics students aspiring for a Ph.D. in this program continued to encounter unusual difficulties gaining acceptance of their dissertation research. In 1930, the completed dissertation of Gladys Anderson was rejected by the administrative committee of the Graduate Council, which asked Schmidt to serve as a referee. He wrote a critique of her thesis expressing doubt that she could have accomplished the work by herself.

> The problems presented [by Anderson's thesis] involve a great deal of labor such as preparation of food, care and feeding of animals, and if adequately carried out, an enormous amount of analytical work. In the writer's opinion, such problems really constitute material for a project requiring the cooperation of several individuals rather than a suitable subject for a beginner in the field of research. Adequate direction would have restricted the candidate's activities to a small portion of this very large and difficult problem.[37]

Morgan responded with disgust that to assume that several individuals would be required for the project "indicates clearly a misunderstanding of the distinction between a problem and a project. What the critic means is that the question attacked is a fundamental one of great importance and is not concerned only with a small detail of a relatively minor problem."[38] She countered:

> In spite of the vague dislike here expressed of our attacking fundamental problems this department must continue this type of research. Small problems slavishly copied from contributions made elsewhere may appear to be safe but are not appealing nor inevitable. We should prefer to withdraw entirely from the research field rather than accept such puerile limitations.[39]

Gladys Anderson finally received her degree from Berkeley in 1932, having won her appeal, and became professor and chair of the home economics department at the University of California at Los Angeles.

After this event Dr. Morgan tried to have Professor Schmidt replaced with another eminent biochemist.

> We beg to relieve us from further annoyance by refraining from appointing Professor Schmidt upon thesis committees from this department. The service of professors from different departments should be reciprocal in this work to be wholesome and this has not been the case between this and biochemistry.[40]

Her strategy was unsuccessful, Dean Lipman pointing out that "if we went picking committees long enough, we could of course get a committee of such a complexion as would pass any thesis."[41] She then sought to gain control over the program by setting up a graduate group in household science, but she was opposed by most faculty in contiguous academic areas, and the effort failed. She expressed disappointment about the rejection in a memo to the dean of the Graduate Division.

> We desire to retain control of the programs and the research of those students who apply to us for guidance in their graduate study. . . . I believe, however, that the staff of this department is competent to judge the fitness of candidates and to guide their studies and to be accorded full autonomy in the matter.[42]

The graduate program of the department never became autonomous; its doctoral students always had to be examined by an interdepartmental group, with their theses always evaluated by outside faculty. Dr. Morgan did devise other means of gaining more control over her program. She devised a new procedure for the qualifying examination of the nutrition candidates, an examination to be held in two parts, one written, one oral. Each member of the committee would submit one question for the written examination, and all answers would be circulated among all members of the committee before the oral examination. This procedure was well received by the members of the interdepartmental nutrition group and by the graduate division as well. In fact, other graduate groups, comparative biochemistry and comparative physiology, for example, adopted a similar procedure soon afterward.

Morgan's last move was to gain appointment as director of the graduate group itself. From 1946 until her retirement in 1954 she remained its head. In 1949 its name was changed from *Animal Nutrition* to *Nutrition*. There were thirty-seven faculty members from three campuses in the group—twenty-one from Berkeley, eleven from Davis, and five from San Francisco. In 1949, eighteen graduate students enrolled; fourteen of them were doctoral candidates.

Altogether, between 1930 and 1962, 31 home economics students earned Ph.D.s in nutrition and 125 earned master's degrees. Most of Dr. Morgan's and Dr. Okey's doctoral students became professors of food science and nutrition at major universities, among them Cornell, Hawaii, Iowa State, Minnesota, Southern California, Tennessee, and the University of California at Los Angeles, Davis, and Berkeley.[43]

Had the department been judged against the criteria of employment of its students, its status would have been very high. This never happened.

When Dr. Okey came to Berkeley in 1919, she was shocked at the poor quality of the department's research facilities (see figure 14). She had come from the Department of Biochemistry at the University of Illinois, one of the best-equipped departments in the country at that time.

> Opportunities for graduate teaching and research were very limited. Our first animal quarters consisted of two packing boxes nailed to the back of our "temporary" frame building. They housed two white rabbits. They were joined later on by another packing box—this one in the basement of the building. It was inhabited by a family of mice contributed by Dr. Sundstroem of Biochemistry, as part of a study of the effect of climate on food consumption and needs. My research budget of $250 was considered generous.[44]

The *San Francisco Chronicle* reported about the inadequate research space:

> "It requires brawn as well as brain to be an instructor in the household science department at the University of California," declare Dr. Lucille Johnson, Dr. Agnes Fay Morgan, and Dr. Ruth Okey, heads of that department on the Berkeley campus. Due to the present fire hazard in the wooden structure which serves as the department's headquar-

ters, the instructors, it was learned yesterday, must carry home each night their records and research results as a precautionary measure.[45]

The article was accompanied by a picture showing the three women lugging their heavy satchels home (see figure 15).

In 1930, when the construction of the new Life Sciences Building was completed, the Department of Household Science finally moved into a permanent building, but even here the research facilities were inadequate (see figure 16).

The Department of Household Science had moved to the Life Sciences Building in 1930/31, with offices and teaching labs on the northwest basement floor and animal quarters on the southeast corner of the fifth floor. Our space in Life Sciences proved to be poorly adapted for our Nutrition work. It was

Figure 14. Analytical Laboratory for Metabolism Research (1923) (Author's private collection)

U. C. Instructors Carrying Home for
Safety Records of Research

` (Left to right) Dr. Lucille Johnson, Dr. Agnes Fay Morgan and Dr. Ruth Okey.

Figure 15. U.C. instructors carrying research records to their homes for safety (1926) (Author's private collection)

crowded, dark, impossible to keep clean, and generally cheerless. My research lab was 50 feet long mostly underground, and had one window. Our much desired animal quarters were badly planned. The unplastered tile partitions were soon alive with various types of vermin—including bedbugs from the shavings used for animal bedding and lice from the swallows who nested in the fifth floor cornices. Ventilation was poor and it was almost impossible to regulate temperature in the south rooms. Our original rat colonies lived in round cages homemade from hardware cloth and set on squares of hardware

cloth over tin cake pans on metal shelving originally designed
for books. . . . Regular janitors refused to work in the animal
rooms. . . . Cages had to be washed in sinks and there was no
provision for sterilization, other than soap and water.[46]

Not only was space lacking, but equipment was as well.
Department members had to depend on other departments for the
use of many instruments. They could, for example, use the micro-
tome, a much-needed instrument for making fine slices of objects
for the microscope, only when it was not in use by other departments. From 1942, because of lack of money, time, and equipment,
Dr. Okey was forced to cease her work on guinea pigs for a period of
more than ten years.[47]

Space is a symbol of power. Those members of the academic
community who have more status are more likely to be successful
in acquiring needed space than those who are less well respected.

Morgan, conscious of status and prestige, in 1944 managed to

Figure 16. Life Science Building: Nutrition research (photo circa 1930)
(University of California Archives)

include a plan for a separate home economics building in the state building program, a plan adopted by the legislature that same year. Five years later detailed plans for the building were completed and construction was scheduled to begin, but due "to some oversight the funding had been delayed."[48] In 1950, funds were appropriated, but because of the Korean War all construction was stopped. In 1952, finally, permission was granted for the building, and only in 1954, the year Dr. Morgan retired, was the four-story building on the northwest end of the campus completed. After ten years of waiting, the department could finally move into its own space (see figure 17). Ironically, half a year later, the Educational Policy Committee of the Academic Senate at Berkeley recommended that the department be moved en bloc to the Davis campus.

But the comfortable new four-story building came too late, in any case, to raise the department's prestige. On the contrary, the seven-room penthouse on the roof designed for home management practice brought the department the reputation of teaching "bed making."[49] See figure 18.

Figure 17. The new Home Economics Building (1954) (Author's private collection)

Faculty service on campus committees indirectly brings status to a department; by participating in a campuswide committee, faculty members become known to colleagues from other departments with whom they would not normally interact. Committee service is a two-way process. Committee members form opinions about each other and also about the department to which they belong. Faculty members gain insight into the inner circle of campus politics and develop an understanding about the goals and objectives of the administration. For department chairs such knowledge is immensely useful. Serving on key campus committees, such as the Academic Senate Budget Committee, the Educational Policy Committee, or the Committee on Committees (which selects faculty for all standing committees), brought access to the administration's plans and protected those departments whose faculty serve on these committees from unwelcome administrative surprises.

Dr. Morgan, as one of the very few female department chairs, became quite visible on the Berkeley campus by following such a

Figure 18. Morgan Hall: View of the home economics laboratory (photo 1954) (University of California Archives)

strategy. Participating in and later directing the interdepartmental Graduate Group in Nutrition, she became known to her male colleagues in related disciplines. She served on many administrative committees as well, but she was never appointed to the most powerful committee, the budget committee. She served on the Committee on Courses, which approved new courses, in this role scrutinizing for several years the offerings of the Department of Education. (Once she recommended that "twenty-seven courses be discontinued" and complained the next year "that instead of discontinuing those courses, four more had been added."[50]) Through these administrative activities she created a name for herself, although not always a very flattering one. Because she spoke out, perhaps more than was expected of a woman, she was remembered by male administrators on campus as a "bitch,"[51] as an "aggressive woman" who "knew black and knew white, but she didn't know much about shades of grey," while "most of us have to deal with greys."[52]

Outside the campus Morgan made a name for herself as a speaker at community events and on radio broadcasts and by publishing widely in a variety of journals, presenting her research results at many conferences. In 1935, for example, she presented a research paper at the International Physiological Congress at Leningrad. In 1936 she presented research reports before the Society for Experimental Biology and Medicine, the American Association for Advancement of Science, the American Chemical Society, the American Society of Biological Chemists, and the American Public Health Association.[53] However, her primary reputation and recognition for service was as a member of the Council of the American Institute of Nutrition (1934) and of the Experiment Station Committee on Organization and Policy of Land-Grant Colleges and as the first woman member of the Committee of Nine, charged with administering cooperative research funds for state Agricultural Experiment Stations (1946–1950).

When she received the Garvan Medal of the American Chemistry Society (an award for women chemists) in 1949 for "distinguished service to chemistry" she did become acknowledged on her own campus.[54] In 1950, the Academic Senate elected her Faculty Research Lecturer, the first time in the history of the Berkeley campus that a woman was nominated for this annual honor, which was bestowed on a Berkeley faculty member "who distinguished himself by scholarly research in his chosen field of study."[55] Even to this day this honor, established under President Wheeler in 1913, has been granted to very few women faculty members (Mary R. Haas in linguistics in 1965, Josephine Miles in English in 1976, Elizabeth Colson in anthropology in 1982, Doris Calloway in nutritional sciences in 1991, Susan Ervin-Tripp in psychology in 1993).

At the award celebration at which she was to speak on her research, Dr. Morgan was excited and apprehensive. Dr. Josephine Smith, for many years a budget officer on campus, remembered the occasion:

> Although she [Dr. Morgan] had often given reports personally to the Regents and even several times exhibits of her nutrition research, she said she had nightmares before the lecture. She thought how awful it would be if nobody came. She was very much on pins and needles, but when the time came there was an overflow audience.[56]

Even so late in her career Morgan did not really dare count on campus recognition. In 1959, after her retirement and after winning other prestigious awards, among them the Borden Award from the American Institute of Nutrition, Morgan received the LL.D., the honorary Doctor of Law degree, from her own university (see figure 19).

As chair, Morgan was the most visible member of the Department of Home Economics, but Professors Ruth Okey and Catherine Landreth, a Ph.D. in psychology from Berkeley who joined the department in 1938 as assistant professor of child development, also became known on campus as outstanding researchers (see figure 20). Okey, a very modest person with a national reputation for her research in biochemistry, was known at Berkeley only to faculty in neighboring disciplines and in the economics department because of her involvement with the Heller Committee in Social Economics (this committee conducted a study to determine the cost of an adequate diet at low cost for people of various ages and families of various sizes). Landreth, who was connected to the Berkeley Institute of Child Welfare, held a joint appointment with the psychology department. During World War II she advised the state on efficient and appropriate housing, staffing, and operating

of child care centers for children of mothers employed in war industries, and after the war she was appointed by the California state
government to undertake a survey on the merits of state support to
child care centers for children of working mothers. This study
received much attention from the state legislature.

Despite the involvement of the faculty of the Department of
Home Economics, and particularly of its chair, with a number of
campus committees, they were not asked to participate in any of
Berkeley's core committees. In 1954, this had serious repercus-
sions, when none of the home economics faculty knew that the
Educational Policy Committee was planning to eliminate home economics altogether as a means of enhancing the university's reputation after the loyalty oath controversy.[57] The home economics

Figure 19. Receiving the honorary Doctor of Law (LL.D.). President Clark
Kerr, Agnes Fay Morgan, Knowles Ryerson (June 11, 1959) (Author's private collection)

Figure 20. Catherine Landreth, Ph.D. psychology, professor of psychology and home economics 1938–1964 (photo 1945) (University of California Archives)

faculty at the time was eagerly planning to expand the department into a full-fledged school of home economics.

A NAME CHANGE AND A FIGHT: WHAT'S IN A NAME? POWER

Throughout the life of any university department, support from the administration is absolutely necessary if the department wants to accomplish any changes. Home economics received only lukewarm support. Claude Hutchison, dean of the College of Agriculture from 1931 through 1952, admitted in an interview that several top administrators, such as Vice President Monroe Deutsch, believed that "home economics was not a proper subject for the university to teach. . . . I believe it would be fair to say that this was a general attitude in the University of California among people who had a lot to do with the university's destiny."[58]

Morgan, ambitious for herself and for the department, tried to stretch the departmental boundaries—for some faculty members on the Berkeley campus, much too far. In 1924 she sought support from President William Campbell to change the name of the department from the Department of Household Science to the Department of Human Nutrition. Campbell, a professor of astronomy, was favorable to the proposal, but concerned about a possible conflict with the Department of Nutrition in the College of Agriculture. Professor Jaffa, nutrition's chair, had no objections since his department concerned itself with animal nutrition only. The dean of the College of Agriculture also had no objections, as he wrote to President Campbell. "There is no objection on the part of Professor Jaffa or myself to the use of the term "Human Nutrition" for the department now called Household Science."[59] President Campbell wrote to Dr. Morgan that he would recommend to the Board of Regents on February 12 the renaming of the department, the name change to take effect on July 1, 1925.[60] However, on March 4, 1924, Dr. Morgan received another note from President Campbell:

> For various reasons, it seems wiser to me that the title DEPARTMENT OF HOUSEHOLD SCIENCE should not be changed to DEPARTMENT OF HUMAN NUTRITION this year. Perhaps the change can be made a year later. I know that this decision will bring some disappointment to you, and I regret that fact.[61]

Carl Schmidt of the Department of Biochemistry had opposed the name change,[62] as had the director of the Agricultural Experiment Station, who reported to the chair of the Committee on Courses:

> Mr. Schmidt feels that establishment of a Department of Human Nutrition would lead to serious difficulties, since human nutrition and nutrition in general is the proper field of biochemistry. From my own work in biochemistry, I think Mr. Schmidt's attitude in this respect is perfectly correct. . . . I

understand that the proposal has been disapproved for the present, and I am confident that it will not be entertained in the future without due consideration.[63]

Dr. Morgan never was content with the name *household science* or *home economics*. At a speech to a joint meeting of the Experiment Station and the home economics research section of the agriculture and home economics division of the Association of the Land-Grant Colleges and Universities at Washington in 1948, she called the name *home economics* "in some ways an inadequate and misleading one. The early connotation with cooking and sewing instruction has lingered erroneously in many minds, even in those of our learned colleagues."[64] In 1953, she wrote in an article published in the *Bulletin* of the American Association of University Professors:

> There is some discontent with the name, Home Economics, for this cluster of subjects. It is incorrect and misleading. . . . Various suggestions have been made as to the desired new name. . . . An entomologist remarked gleefully that it is too bad the zoologists and entomologists have snapped up Ecology, since "Human Ecology" might fill the bill.[65]

In 1960, the remainder of the former Department of Home Economics and Food Science and Technology were combined, along with the food science laboratory of the Institute of Marine Resources, and the newly organized department was called "Nutritional Science." With the change in name came also a change of the name of the Home Economics Building. The new chair, Professor George Briggs, hired to reorganize the department, requested immediately such a change for the building, suggesting Morgan Hall. On the one hand, it would recognize Dr. Morgan's outstanding contribution in the field of nutrition, and, on the other hand, it would be a tactical move to appease the home economics community in California, outraged at the elimination of home economics at Berkeley. Briggs admitted as much:

> It now becomes very urgent that the building be re-named, effective as soon as possible, as an important aid to the establishment and public acceptance of the revised "Department of

Nutritional Sciences," as we are expected to be called. As you know, all other divisions of the field of home economics are leaving this campus on July 1, or sooner. . . . In addition, naming the building after Dr. Morgan will do much to help soothe the many Home Economics forces in this State who have regretted the moving of the other divisions of home economics to the Davis Campus. It will make the transition much easier. Dr. Morgan, as you know, was Chairman of the Department from 1918 to 1954, and has an international reputation as a nutritionist and home economist.[66]

In addition, with a man now in charge of the department, the designation *home economics* became an embarrassment and an impediment to grants. George Briggs explained to the dean of natural resources:

This urgency is necessary because the present name is not only outdated and not indicative of the change in emphasis to nutrition, but at times the old name has actually proven embarrassing. As an example of the latter, we are soon to present an application to the U.S. Public Health Service for matching grants for construction of the nutrition laboratories in this building. Our chances of getting this grant would be very slim indeed if it were indicated on the application that this is called a "Home Economics Building."[67]

On March 22, 1962, the university celebrated the renaming of the building as Morgan Hall (see figure 21). It was the first, and still the only, building on the Berkeley campus named for a woman recognized because of her own academic achievements and not because of donations to the university.

This surely must have been a day of triumph for Agnes Fay Morgan. But it was also a slap in the face. When Dr. Morgan had requested that the name of her department be changed, her request was rejected; she had to live for thirty-six years with the old name. Now, when a man requested that the name be changed, the request was granted. The reorganized Department of Nutritional Sciences maintained all the areas Dr. Morgan had developed—nutrition, foods, and dietetics—and disposed of those areas that the state Department of Education had insisted that the

department offer—teacher training in home economics and training of home economics extension workers. Perhaps in her seventies
Morgan had developed a thick enough skin to be able to enjoy her
dream of a Department of Nutrition now finally true. In 1965, in
her closing remarks at the symposium honoring her fiftieth
anniversary at the university, Morgan showed how aware she was
of the importance of the name of a field and the connotation it car-
ries: "If we could find some way of adding the word 'molecular' to
our department name we might be able to command more prestige,
funds and followers."[68]

Gender and status form a vicious circle. Morgan had tried
every strategy to raise the status of the department—hiring
instructors with Ph.D.s, developing a science-dominated curriculum, undertaking numerous research projects and publishing
widely, trying to secure outside research funds, developing a Ph.D.

Figure 21. Renaming the Home Economics Building to Morgan Hall,
A. F. Morgan and her son Arthur Morgan (March 12, 1962) (Author's
private collection)

program and placing the department's students well, and securing space and visibility on campus. However, every strategy she tried had a specific gendered edge to it. A strong science-oriented curriculum conflicted with the demands from the state Department of Education for more practical teacher training for home economics teachers for secondary schools. The research topics she and her staff chose out of need for textbooks, money, space, and research subjects dealt with problems of women and children. They were need-oriented and hence perceived as less fundamental than research topics chosen by men. Morgan did not succeed in changing the name of her department supposedly since the more accurate name would have intruded too much into territories accepted as men's fields of research. Home economics was a field for women, and women should stay there or disappear altogether. Women students who majored in home economics were assumed to be lacking research originality and analytical skills, as the early members of the graduate group in animal nutrition demonstrated. Being outspoken in administrative committees and protesting exceptional treatment, Morgan was remembered as aggressive, not conciliatory. Finally, the visibility gained by the construction of the Home Economics Building made other faculty on campus mock the penthouse for home management training, and the department was again perceived as a trade school department.

The fact that Morgan was elected faculty research lecturer and awarded an honorary degree on her own campus was due solely to her extraordinary capabilities both in research and in administrative matters. As Rossiter said, "any but the most extraordinary" were advanced and promoted.[69] Arlie Hochschild, professor of sociology at Berkeley, further wrote that such an extraordinary woman needed not only "to be more dedicated, reliable and productive *than men* to get the same recognition," but she must also be "more dedicated, reliable, and productive than what people in general and employers in particular expect *other women* in the profession to be."[70] Only then can such a woman receive her due.

Because they were women, Agnes Fay Morgan and Ruth Okey, together with other women who were similarly trained in chemistry, could not find employment in departments of chemistry or biochemistry. Segregated into home economics departments, these exceptional women chemists had no access to research money other than funds specifically designated for problems concerning food, family, children, and women. Professional associations such as the American Institute of Nutrition and many universities did not value this kind of research.

Given the research produced by the Department of Home Economics and the successful employment of its students, the department should have ranked high in status on the Berkeley campus, but it did not. Its chair, Agnes Fay Morgan, gained status and recognition on campus, but she could gain and hold it only for herself.

CHAPTER 5

FROM "THE PEAK OF EMINENCE"
TO THE END OF A SEPARATE SPHERE:
BERKELEY FINDS HOME ECONOMICS
AN EMBARRASSMENT

In July 1954, on the occasion of Agnes Fay Morgan's retirement after thirty-six years as chair of the Berkeley Department of Home Economics, President Gordon Sproul wrote to her: "You have brought our Department of Home Economics up the long trail from the first courses in scientific nutrition to the peak of eminence it now occupies in the nation."[1]

Exactly one year later, in June 1955, the Berkeley faction of the northern section of the Academic Senate Committee on Educational Policy proposed that home economics at Berkeley be abolished altogether and the entire department moved to Davis, then in the process of becoming a fully independent campus of the University of California. The Davis administration at first rejected the offer, urging Berkeley to keep home economics.[2] But a year later, in May, the northern section of the Committee on Educational

Policy of the university (the Berkeley and Davis campuses) unanimously recommended that the Department of Home Economics be transported to Davis. The recommendation was accepted with alacrity and relief by the Berkeley administration, the vice president of agricultural sciences for all the campuses of the university, the president, and the regents. Departmental reorganization promptly began, with nutritional sciences severed from home economics and retained by the Berkeley campus. Food science, food technology, and the Marin Food Laboratory were merged with nutritional science. In 1960, George Briggs was hired to implement the move of home economics to Davis and to head Berkeley's newly prestigious Department of Nutritional Sciences. In 1962 the Home Economics Building, completed only in 1954, was renamed A. F. Morgan Hall, an ironic tribute to Agnes Fay Morgan whose organizational work the new plan dismantled. With this name change, the last vestige of home economics at Berkeley disappeared.

The decision to dismantle the department had been made wholly without consulting the faculty of the department or the dean of the College of Agriculture in which it was housed. The department faculty were simply invited to present a report, on November 2, 1955, on the department's plans for the next five years before the Chancellor's Academic Advisory Committee, whereupon they were informed that several university committees engaged in general planning efforts had concluded that the Berkeley department ought to be dispatched to the Davis campus. There, it was argued, in the neighborhood of other agriculturally related departments on a rapidly expanding campus, a strong home economics department could develop in an environment more traditionally conducive to home economics training. Morgan's interim successor, acting chair and professor Jessie Coles, resigned in the light of these developments, writing on November 7, 1955, in cold disgust to the vice president of agricultural services:

> At the time I accepted the chairmanship, which, as you know, I did with great reluctance, it was with the belief that there was an opportunity to develop the potentialities this campus affords for an outstanding Department of Home Economics. There was no indication at the time that the Administration was not also looking forward to such a development. A new building had just been completed. A committee had been

appointed to recommend a suitable person for the chairmanship of the Department. Another had been asked to report on
the advisability of establishing a School of Home Economics.
Members of the Department were encouraged to propose new
curricula. Yet about three months after assuming my duties I
was informed for the first time that the Administration entertained serious doubts as to the place of Home Economics on
the Berkeley campus.[3]

The response from the vice president of agricultural sciences to
Coles was a brief three sentences of polite and cool regret, with a
concluding note of business: "I am sorry that you feel compelled to
resign as chairman of the Home Economics Department on the
Berkeley campus. However, I appreciate your willingness to carry
on the routine business of the department until a successor is
appointed. A successor will be appointed when the Dean of the
College of Agriculture returns."[4]

The dean of the Berkeley College of Agriculture, Knowles
Ryerson, had also been left in ignorance of the administration's
intentions to eliminate home economics at the Berkeley campus.
Years later Ryerson complained with exasperation:

As the Dean responsible for that college, I had a right to know
what they were planning. . . . As I told Kerr when I sought an
explanation. . . even worse, you've got a committee who never
even gave the home ec staff the courtesy of sitting down with
them and discussing their problems and getting their views. A
couple of the committee members walked through the building
one day with several staff members and didn't even sit down, I
was told. They only asked a few questions and then came out
with a recommendation to abolish the whole thing. The
Academic Senate wouldn't have dared do that if it had been a
men's faculty. You'd have had an uproar to defend academic
privilege, charges of discourtesy, and all this kind of thing.[5]

Receiving support for home economics and recognition of unfair
treatment by the academic senate committee from a male member
of the administration was exceptional. Ryerson, himself, had been
subjected to unexpected administrative changes in 1952, when he
was ousted from running the fledgling Davis campus as director of

the branch of the College of Agriculture, because President Sproul appointed a close personal friend, Stanley Freeborn, as provost of Davis. Ryerson was cognizant of behind-the-door administrative wheeling and dealing, and he could readily sympathize with the home economics faculty. Connecting sex discrimination with the academic senate committee's behavior is probably attributable to the time (1977) in which his oral history interview was recorded. By this time the women's movement had revealed sex discrimination patterns in higher education institutions and statements such as Ryerson's were no longer anomalies.

Ryerson's support of home economics was derived from a view that home and family are the core of society and that the university, in its mission to serve society, has an obligation to be invested in home and family life.

If this University is to contribute to the life of the people of this state it had better be interested in the quality of home life. It is pretty basic science, especially if you consider the present divorce rate. . . . Too many people think of home economics in terms of cooking and sewing, but it is basic to public health, to pre-med work, and to many other things.[6]

Ryerson was a force in lobbying for retaining the nutritional science part of the department in Berkeley.

How can the administration's decision to discontinue home economics at Berkeley be explained? Several factors came into play.

During the first decade of the century, the Department of Home Economics at Berkeley was created as a means of coping with the many women enrolled at the university by resorting to the prevailing ideology of separate spheres for men and women. In this model, women were to receive a higher education in order to become better wives and mothers but not to compete professionally with men. The women faculty and women students, however, sought to build their new department as an academic discipline that would broaden the employment opportunities for college-educated women, chemists by training. Along with many other women pioneers in science, these women were unable to gain academic employment in their own field of study. The head of the department for thirty-six years had built it along basic scientific lines. Yet the department was not allowed to name itself according to its central activity—human nutrition. Outside pressures from the California State Department of Education, the pressures of two wars, the Depression, and lack of support from the university administration had forced the department to offer traditional women's courses, such as institutional management and household economics in 1932; dietetics in 1935; child development, textiles, and clothing in 1938; and family sociology in 1950.

Research funds were minimal and laboratory space meager, yet the core members of the department, Morgan and Okey, succeeded in producing outstanding nutrition research. As an individual Morgan received recognition for her work, but her department was not accorded credit. In fact, right after her retirement in 1954, her department was criticized by campus and universitywide academic senate committees for requiring too many science courses, a criticism highly inconsistent with Berkeley's own standards. But as long as Morgan headed the department, basic science teaching and research within home economics did dominate, tolerated by the campus administration. But after she retired the department was forced to shift its focus to helping women students prepare for family life rather than the world of science.

Over the course of its existence, the department seemed doomed regardless of the direction in which it moved. On the one hand, in its undergraduate program it was attacked for requiring too many science courses and for not offering course work "appropriate" to women. The Committee on Educational Policy argued that this over-emphasis on science discouraged women from entering the program.[7] Berkeley—one of the largest California state universities—was producing too few home economics teachers and thus failed to meet the state's needs. And, because of its professional curricular outlook, home economics at Berkeley was criticized further for offering an inadequate liberal arts education for those women students who were at the university for a general liberal arts education only.

On the other hand, the department was criticized for not preparing graduate students rigorously enough for a scientific career. The same Educational Policy Committee that accused home economics of having too professional an outlook on its undergraduate curriculum proposed to eliminate all graduate education in home economics, because during the "increasing specialization" of graduate education the student is "drawn closer to the fundamental disciplines which underlie her subject." The committee argued that students doing "research in nutrition should depend very heavily on the medical and biological sciences; a graduate student in consumer economics would need to develop her knowledge of economics. Thus advanced work leads back to some already established basic disciplines, and such work would be better done within the department devoted to that basic discipline."[8] Distancing the campus from applied disciplines and moving more and more "towards basic research in every field" were major goals of the chancellorship at Berkeley between 1952 and 1958, as Clark Kerr has explained.

The 1955 decision to discontinue home economics at Berkeley came at a time when the loyalty oath controversy of 1949 to 1951 had shaken up the campus as it would the nation.[9] In its wake some of the "best men on the faculty" resigned and went elsewhere.[10] In response, Kerr, as the new Berkeley chancellor in 1952, made restoration of faculty confidence and the reestablishment of Berkeley's place among top-ranking universities the major objectives of his administration. He required every department to prepare a "five- and ten-year expectation" report and commissioned all academic senate committees to review systematically Berkeley's academic programs in order to see how best the campus could improve. According to Kerr, the Committee on Educational Policy, the Academic Senate Budget Committee, the Committee on Courses, and the Chancellor's Academic Advisory Committee, "Home Economics was not an area where we could ever distinguish ourselves, and we were looking for ways to distinguish ourselves."[11]

Another reason for the criticism of the department—not by the new campus administration, but by some of the old-guard faculty— was the dominant ideology of the 1950s that liberal arts provides the best education for the many contingencies of women's lives.[12] Since "ninety percent of college girls were going to be mothers in due time," preparation for family life would be the most appropriate role higher education could play for women.[13] General home economics, with its various subfields of food, clothing, child development, and consumer economics, based on the physical, biological, and social sciences, as well as on the arts and humanities, was regarded as a proper basis for a sound liberal arts education, but until Morgan's retirement these aspects of home economics, and particularly those based on social sciences and the arts, played a secondary role in the course offerings of the department.

Faculty and others who believed in the importance of home economics as a field for women argued nonetheless that one such department among the northern campuses of the University of California was enough. Davis would be the ideal place for a strong home economics program since many of the applied arts, including agriculture, were already ensconced on that campus.

Behind the argument for the move to Davis was also a very utilitarian motive: Berkeley desperately needed more space as well as more prestige. Student enrollment had increased by 11 percent, to nearly 22,500, from 1940 until 1950 (see table 5.1). Research facilities had expanded, and many departments were housed in cramped rooms. "A transfer of the Home Economics program to Davis would help relieve the present overcrowding of space at Berkeley," said the vice president of agricultural sciences, an argument impossible to resist.[14] Space that the department had occupied could be made available for more prestigious departments.

A final reason that contributed to the administration's decision to move home economics to Davis was a 1953 statewide *Restudy of*

Table 5.1:   Enrollment by Sex at the University of California, Berkeley, between 1920 and 1962

Year	Men	Women	Total	%Women
1920	5,850	4,496	10,346	43%
1925	5,739	4,749	10,488	45%
1930	6,361	5,463	11,824	46%
1935	8,774	5,644	14,418	39%
1940	10,602	6,411	17,013	38%
1945	10,247	8,015	18,262	44%
1950	15,851	6,495	22,346	29%
1955	12,935	6,241	19,176	33%
1960	15,745	8,229	23,974	34%
1962	17,609	9,861	27,470	36%

Source: Verne Stadtman, ed., *The Centennial Record of the University of California* (1967): 214–24.

the Needs of California in Higher Education commissioned by the state legislature.[15] This study, which eventually laid the foundation for the California Master Plan in Higher Education in the 1960s, reviewed home economics education in all California institutions of higher education. On the study team which prepared background material for the home economics section were nine persons from the California state colleges, including one person from the University of California, Gladys Everson, chair of the Davis Home Economics Department. No one from the Berkeley department, the most established home economics department in California, was even invited to participate.

The restudy's final report, written by the joint staff of the university and the state Department of Education under a chief consultant, T. R. McConnell,[16] concluded that home economics was a highly expensive field of study requiring an expensive building and facilities with specialized laboratories for each of its subfields: food, nutrition, home management, child development, and textile and clothing analysis. It recommended, therefore, that the "placement of such programs should be done with careful considerations"[17] and that "the University of California should review the offerings in home economics on all its campuses with the purpose of effecting coordination and economy of operation."[18]

The Berkeley campus administration took these recommendations as a welcome excuse for expelling home economics from Berkeley. That the newly completed, $1.5 million building was specifically designed for the special needs of home economics training and that more money would have to be spent to refit the building for the needs of a different department were not arguments in favor of retaining the department, or so the Educational Policy Committee thought.[19] The logic of such an argument would be inconsistent with both the state's goals and also the university's obligation to optimize resources, because Davis would need to greatly expand its quarters and laboratory equipment to accommodate the Berkeley department. The Davis program had developed as a branch of the Berkeley department in 1945 and had been administered by the Berkeley chair. Until 1954 Davis had offered only a general, nondegree home economics (home making) program and an undergraduate home economics teachers program. Although Morgan objected to the university being in vocational training, she went along with the more vocational home economics training at Davis. It had a brand new building, but one smaller than Berkeley's, and it lacked the sophisticated set-up and lab equipment.

Once the consideration of moving the Berkeley home economics department to Davis became public (the *Oakland Tribune* reported it on December 15, 1955), protest letters from numerous professional associations—the various home economics and dietetic associations, faculty for home economics departments, and various parent-teacher associations—poured into the chancellor's and the president's offices. These letters, and also a series of meetings between these outside groups and the administration, forced the university to acknowledge its department's "high national reputation for research and graduate work in the field of human nutrition."[20] Vice President for Agricultural Sciences Harry R. Wellman, with much input from Berkeley's Dean of Agriculture Knowles Ryerson, suggested that Berkeley "keep the same type of program at the research and graduate level as Professor Agnes Fay Morgan developed."[21] However, it would not be a home economics program. The Educational Policy Committee agreed and further suggested that a search for a "top flight nutritionist" to replace Dr. Morgan begin.

In the end, the more prestigious nutrition portion of the home economics department at Berkeley was appropriated and integrated into the university's male-dominated fields of food science and food technology. It was not sent on to Davis; the Berkeley administration had its cake and ate it, too. With this move, the composition of the faculty in the new Department of Nutritional Sciences changed from 91 percent female to 31 percent female between 1954 and 1968, and the leadership was wholly male (see figure 22).

Berkeley had decided to retain nutrition for another reason: nutrition research had grown in status after the war. In 1940 the American Food and Nutrition Board was founded as part of the National Research Council under the umbrella of the National Academy of Sciences. The National Science Foundation, the National Institutes of Health, and the National Institute for Mental Health, which had become the main supporters of academic research after World War II, financed research on nutrition but did not recognize home economics as a field of science, although nutrition was a key subfield of home economics.[22] On the international level, the United Nations established the World Health Organization and funds for nutrition research had become available. Once money was to be gotten, men moved into the field. What had once been a female-dominated field became more male-dominated. With the increase of status in this field, it, correspondingly, became of interest to the Berkeley administration. Nutritional science (without home economics, teacher training, institutional management, textiles, or clothing) had the potential to contribute to the upgrading of the Berkeley campus's reputation.

The new planning philosophy of the 1950s, based upon the principles of efficiency and merit, disregarded both the particular history of women scientists at Berkeley and the realities and attitudes toward women in the university and in the labor market. Although officially women had unrestricted access to all academic fields and professions, in reality they faced great resistance whenever they sought to enroll in programs outside liberal arts or home economics. In 1951, for example, the male Nobel laureate and chair

Figure 22. Department of Nutritional Sciences (1962) (Author's private collection)

of the biochemistry department at Berkeley told a returning woman student that she had "better go home and produce more babies."[23] Eliminating home economics at Berkeley meant eliminating a field of study which in the past had been virtually the only easily accessible discipline for women with an interest in science. It further meant eliminating a field where women could advance professionally with the same ease and career possibilities as men and where women could occupy leadership positions. In 1950, out of the 1,072 tenured faculty at Berkeley, 43 were women. In 1968, out of 1,237 tenured faculty, 44 were women, 4 of whom were in nutritional science. The percentage of tenured women faculty members among all tenured faculty declined on the Berkeley campus from a high of 6.0 percent in 1950 to a low of 3.5 percent in 1968.

The fate of the Berkeley Department of Home Economics was not unique among similar programs at major research universities. When many of the well-established leaders in the field were ready to retire in the 1950s and 1960s, top research universities around the country used the opportunity to reorganize, reduce, or disband home economics programs altogether, although these programs produced the largest numbers of home economics Ph.D.s in the country. The University of Chicago's home economics program—one of the most respected in the country—was terminated in 1956.[24] Columbia University's Teacher College Department of Home Economics was reorganized in the late 1940s and early 1950s to become a subordinate program within the Department of Science Education. Part of Pennsylvania State University's College of Home Economics was dispersed to other colleges. What remained was renamed the "College of Human Development" and was headed by a male psychologist in 1968.[25] West Virginia University separated home economics from the College of Agriculture and moved it into the new College of Education and Human Resources, headed by a man.[26] Cornell University's New York State College of Home Economics was dramatically reorganized after its dean retired in 1968 and a man with no previous experience in home economics became the new dean of the renamed College of Human Ecology.[27]

Often these changes occurred when ambitious presidents, urged by aggressive boards of trustees, were eager to distance themselves from any perception of being a "cow college" and tried to turn their institutions overnight into prestigious universities.[28] These presidents found home economics baffling and an embarrassment. Young male deans and department chairs were hired to straighten out the newly created configurations.

Hand in hand with the reorganization of home economics programs went a drastic reduction of women faculty in the newly created departments and an inverse increase in male faculty. Again, the changes at Berkeley were not isolated ones. For example, the proportion of female to male faculty members at the College of Home Economics at Pennsylvania State (renamed "Human Development" in 1968) dropped from 75 percent to 50 percent, with the proportion of male faculty increasing from 25 percent to 50 percent between 1965 and 1972. At Cornell, the proportion of women to men faculty members in what had been home economics changed from 82 percent female to 62 percent female and from 18 percent male to 38 percent male between 1965 and 1972.[29] Home economics, the stronghold of women in science, was seriously undermined and eventually disappeared on many campuses.

Two clear lines of gender stratification existed within the University of California: the first, at the turn of the century, was a product of the societal ideology of a separate sphere for women and brought open and unequal stratification. The second form of gender stratification, which occurred in the early 1950s during the reorganization of higher education in California, furthered covert stratification of the university via academic status and prestige. Women were irrevocably associated with low-status, low-prestige departments. Home economics had never been allowed to develop much status, and any prestige accumulated by individuals within the department adhered only to them and was never transferred to the department as a whole. Finally, and ironically, the most scientifically sound aspect of home economics, its core research in human nutrition, which was the women scholars' original principal interest, but frowned upon by male administrators, was moved out of the department by the university administration as soon as its prestige rose. Home economics, without nutrition, was low in status. It simply had to go.

Conclusion

Lessons

Seven principal lessons can be learned from this book. First, new programs need strong political and professional allies outside the university who are able to impose pressure on the university administration. Beginning in 1909, Berkeley women, both students and faculty, relied heavily on outside allies, such as the Federation of California Women's Clubs, the Berkeley Town and Gown Club, and the Association of University Women, to write to the president urging the administration to establish a home economics department. In 1955 the protests from outside groups such as the California Home Economics and Dietetics Associations, Parent-Teacher Associations, faculty from other home economics departments at research universities, and alumnae were successful in forcing the administration to reconsider its plan and to retain human nutrition research and its graduate program on the Berkeley campus.

Second, any new program must garner allies on its own campus, and all new programs must make a serious effort to become known on campus.[1] This means that faculty and students in other departments generally must understand the content of what is taught and what kind of research is undertaken by its faculty. For example, in the case of home economics, there was a historical mis-understanding between the concepts of 'bed making' and 'nutrition research.' Clark Kerr, chancellor in 1954 when the fate of the home economics department was being debated in Berkeley's academic senate committees, understood home economics simply as the place where they teach "bed making" and offer courses that cover "in ten easy lectures. . . courtship to venereal diseases." (He referred to popular family sociology courses offered in home economics at that time.)[2]

Third, it does not pay for a newly established department to hire stars alone as faculty; recognition may be attributed only to them and not to the department as a whole. The honor accorded Morgan—appointment as faculty research lecturer, the highest academic honor the Berkeley Academic Senate bestows upon a faculty member—did not bring status to her department.

Fourth, new programs need to walk a fine line between establishing a program with rigorous academic requirements and over-burdening the program for fear of being regarded as unscientific and not being taken seriously. A recent study of time to doctoral degree on the nine University of California campuses found that all newly created doctoral programs appear to require an unusual number of exams and specifications compared to the practice in older, established programs.[3] A program overburdened with requirements can easily be criticized as having an incoherent curriculum.

Fifth, newly developed university programs should strive to establish their own Ph.D. programs. At a research university, only a doctoral program brings a national and international reputation, which translates into higher status for the department. In spite of many attempts, the home economics department at Berkeley was never allowed to have its own doctoral program, and the students who had an interest in graduate research had to get their degrees in the Interdisciplinary Graduate Group in Nutrition.

Sixth, higher education scholars will have an incomplete analysis if they do not include gender as an important factor in studies of university history and the way in which a university functions, as well as in biographies of the university's leaders.

Finally, for women, the hard-learned lesson of home economics at Berkeley demonstrates that women scholars do not necessarily succeed by adopting conventional university values. At Berkeley, the home economics department was first doomed when it adhered to stringent academic standards for its graduates and then marked with low status when it did not have its own Ph.D. program. Women who forge into an organization, such as a university, dominated by men should dare to be unconventional and stand up for their own goals and values.

APPENDIX

A CHRONOLOGICAL HISTORY OF HOME ECONOMICS AT THE UNIVERSITY OF CALIFORNIA, BERKELEY

ADMINISTRATION	HOME ECONOMICS	OTHER DEPARTMENTS
President Benjamin Ide Wheeler (1899–1919)	1905 First home economics courses offered in domestic science and cookery	
Dean of Women Lucy Sprague (1906–1912)		
	1909 Wheeler sets up Committee on Domestic Science chaired by Jessica Peixotto Ellen Swallow Richards teaches summer session courses "Household Management in the Twentieth Century—Relation of Cost to Efficiency" and "Euthenics"	1909 University Farm School opens at Davis

ADMINISTRATION	HOME ECONOMICS	OTHER DEPARTMENTS
	1910 Dr. Sophonisba Breckinridge teaches summer session courses "Public Aspects of the Household" and "Legal and Economic Position of Women"	
	1911 The Prytaneans, women's honor society, petitions President Wheeler for classes in home economics	
	1912 Mary Kissell hired as associate professor of domestic art	1912 University Extension School of Jurisprudence (law school) opens
Dean of Women Lucy Ward Stebbins (1913–1941)	1913 Committee on Domestic Science becomes Committee on Home Economics under Professor Jaffa's chairmanship	
	1914 Mary Kissell resigns Mary Patterson appointed assistant professor of domestic art Agnes Fay Morgan appointed assistant professor of nutrition	1914 Agricultural Extension Service School of Education opens
	1915 January, A. F. Morgan's appointment at Berkeley begins	

ADMINISTRATION	HOME ECONOMICS	OTHER DEPARTMENTS
	1916 Department of Home Economics opened in the College of Liberal Arts and Sciences with subdivisions in household art and household science, department chaired by Mary Patterson Provisional Home Economics Building constructed	
	1917–1918 A. F. Morgan organizes volunteer program requested by United Food Administration for war effort	
	1918 Home economics department splits into two divisions that soon become departments: 1. Household science, chaired by A. F. Morgan 2. Household arts, chaired by Mary Patterson	
President David Scott Barrows (1919–1923)	**1919** Ruth Okey (Ph.D. chemistry, Illinois) hired as assistant professor A. F. Morgan becomes associate professor	
President William Wallace Campbell (1923–1929)	**1923** A. F. Morgan becomes full professor Birth of Morgan's son, Arthur	
		1926 School of Librarianship

ADMINISTRATION	HOME ECONOMICS	OTHER DEPARTMENTS
	1930 Household science moves to the new Life Sciences Building in the College of Agriculture Department becomes Department of Home Economics Interdepartmental graduate group in (animal) nutrition established; chaired by Carl Schmidt, professor of biochemistry (1930–1946)	
Dean of the College of Agriculture Claude Hutchinson (1931–1952)	**1931** A. F. Morgan's first trip to Europe to visit nutrition research labs	
	1932 New courses: 1. Household science: institutional management, hospital dietetics 2. Household art: interior design, home management, consumer education	
	1936 A. F. Morgan's second trip abroad to present a paper on vitamin D at the Leningrad Physiological Conference	
	1938 Catherine Landreth (psychologist) hired as assistant professor	
Dean of Women Mary Blossom Davis (1940–1951)		**1944** School of Public Health opens School of Social Welfare opens

ADMINISTRATION	HOME ECONOMICS	OTHER DEPARTMENTS
	1945 Home economics programs at U.C. Davis developed as a branch of Berkeley campus department, administered by A. F. Morgan	
	1946 A. F. Morgan becomes director of the interdepartmental graduate group in nutrition	
	1949 A. F. Morgan receives Garvan Medal from the American Chemical Society	
	1950–1951 A. F. Morgan named Faculty Research Lecturer at U.C. Berkeley	**1950** School of Criminology opens **1951** U.C. Davis opens the College of Letters and Science
Chancellor at Berkeley Clark Kerr (1952–1957) Vice President for Agricultural Science Harry Wellman (1952–1958) Dean of the College of Agriculture Knowles Ryerson (1952–1960)	**1954** A. F. Morgan retires; department moves to new Home Economics Building Jessie Coles (economist) becomes chair of the Department of Home Economics	

ADMINISTRATION	HOME ECONOMICS	OTHER DEPARTMENTS
T. R. McConnell, Chief Consultant for the Master Plan for Higher Education 1953	1955 University administration decides to move home economics to U.C. Davis Jessie Coles resigns Ruth Okey becomes department chair University administration decides to leave the nutritional science component of home economics at Berkeley	
President Clark Kerr (1958–1967)		
	1960 George Briggs becomes chair of the new Department of Nutritional Sciences consisting of the nutritional science component of the old home economics department, food science, food technology, and the Food Science Laboratory of the Institute of Marine Resources Department of Home Economics moves to U.C. Davis except the nutritional science component (A. F. Morgan's research focus)	
Chancellor at Berkeley Edward William Strong (1961–1965)	1962 University celebrates the renaming of the Home Economics Building as Morgan Hall Last home economics students graduate	

ADMINISTRATION	HOME ECONOMICS	OTHER DEPARTMENTS
	1963 A. F. Morgan receives the Phoebe Hearst Gold Medal as one of the ten outstanding women in the San Francisco Bay Area	
	1968 A. F. Morgan dies	

NOTES

INTRODUCTION

1. See Helen Lefkowitz Horowitz, "Does Gender Bend the History of Higher Education?" *American Literary History* 7, no. 2 (summer 1995): 344–49.

2. Gloria Bowles and Renate D. Klein, eds., *Theories of Women's Studies* (London: Routledge and Kegan Paul, 1983).

3. See also Geraldine J. Clifford and James W. Guthrie, *Ed. School: A Brief for Professional Education* (Chicago: University of Chicago Press, 1988).

4. Emma Willard (1787–1879); Mary Lyon (1797–1849); and Catherine Beecher (1800–1878).

5. Jane Bernard Powers, *The "Girl Question" in Education: Vocational Education for Young Women in the Progressive Era* (London: The Falmer Press, 1992).

6. Laura Shapiro, *Perfection Salad: Women and Cooking at the Turn of the Century* (New York: Farrar, Straus and Giroux, 1986), Charlotte Perkins Gilman (1860–1935), a feminist, author and lecturer, who embraced socialist ideas, also believed that science could relieve women from housework and free their position in society.

7. One of the most famous cooking schools was the Boston Cooking School. Organized by the Women's Education Association of Boston in 1879, it was an off-spring of the women's club movement. Fannie Merritt Farmer (1857–1915), whose name is still famous today, was its director

from 1891 through 1902. During her tenure, she published the *Boston Cooking School Book* (1896), later better known as the *Fannie Farmer's Book of Good Dinners*. Her books, although rewritten and revised, are still in print today. Another well-known cooking school was the New York Cooking School, begun by Juliet Corson in 1876.

8. Karen J. Blair, *The Clubwomen as Feminist* (New York: Holmes and Meier Publishers, 1980). They believed in the idea of municipal housekeeping, meaning that "women's function, like charity, begins at home and then, like charity, goes everywhere."

9. See more on the idea that women should have the same rigorous education as men in Barbara M. Solomon, *In the Company of Educated Women* (New Haven: Yale University Press, 1985), and Florence Howe, *Myths of Coeducation: Selected Essays, 1964–1983* (Bloomington: Indiana University Press, 1984).

10. Lake Placid Conference on Home Economics: Proceedings of the First Annual Conference (Lake Placid, New York, 1899), 7.

11. Lake Placid Conference on Home Economics: Proceedings of the Fourth Annual Conference (Lake Placid, New York, 1902), 70–71.

12. Lake Placid Conference on Home Economics: Proceedings of the Eighth Annual Conference (Lake Placid: New York, 1906), 33.

13. Isabel Bevier, Catharine F. Langworthy, and Mary Urie Watson were nominated as vice presidents; Benjamin R. Andrew, later professor of household economics, Teachers College, Columbia, became secretary-treasurer.

14. Henrietta Calvin and Carrie A. Lyford.

15. Isabel Bevier, *Home Economics in Education*, 2nd ed. (1924; reprinted Philadelphia: J. B. Lippincott, 1928), 173.

16. As quoted by Earl Cheit, *The Useful Arts and the Liberal Tradition* (New York: McGraw-Hill Book Company, 1975), 44.

17. Surprisingly, the AHEA did not lobby to include home economics in the bill; it was rather the General Federation of Women's Clubs that did so. Only after the draft bill stated that only one-fifth of the trade and industrial appropriations could be used for home economics did the AHEA zealously work for equal funding of home economics education.

18. See also: Cheit, *Useful Arts*.

19. I participated in this celebration on 28 January 1985.

20. In her book, *Women of Ideas and What Men Have Done to Them:*

From Aphra Behn to Adrienne Rich (London: Routledge and Kegan Paul, 1982), Dale Spender shows how common this experience is to women.

21. George Briggs, chair of the restructured home economics department from 1962 through 1970, kept these materials in boxes under his study table. He kindly gave me access to them, and it greatly enriched this work. Also, there is virtually no material on Jessica Peixotto, the second woman Ph.D. and the first woman full professor at Berkeley. However, the archives do have considerable material on her father and her brother, such as personal scrapbooks, family albums, and so on.

22. Dr. Gloria Bowles was the coordinator of the program from 1976 until 1983.

23. A successful beginning to the dialogue between women's studies scholars and home economists occurred in October 1991, at a conference at Cornell University entitled: "Rethinking Women and Home Economics in the 20th Century." Its contributions countered the notion that home economics was nothing more than "glorified housekeeping." See Sara Stage and Virginia Vincenti, *Rethinking Home Economics* (Cornell: Cornell University Press, 1997).

CHAPTER 1

1. *Summer Session University of California Bulletin*, 6, no. 3: 57–58.

2. *The Record*, no. 4, 6 July 1905 (University of California Archives, Bancroft Library at the University of California, Berkeley): 1.

3. Contrary to common belief, the University of California did not start out as a coeducational institution, as did most land-grant colleges and as the history of higher education assumes. See Mabel Newcomer, *A Century of Higher Education for American Women* (New York: Harper and Brothers, 1959); Thomas Woody, *A History of Women's Education in the United States*, vol. 2 (New York: Science Press, 1929); and Solomon, *In the Company of Educated Women* (New Haven: Yale University Press, 1985). *The Act to Create and Organize the University of California of 1868*, which can be found in the archival records of the university, states that "any resident of California of the age of fourteen years and upwards, of approved moral character, shall have the right to enter himself in the University as a student at large." It does not speak about admitting women. In fact, during the first year of the university's existence, thirty-eight male students registered and were taught by a faculty of ten men.

4. The *Register of the University of 1870* for the first time mentioned under terms of admission: "YOUNG LADIES.—Young Ladies are admitted into the University on equal terms, in all respects with young men." No further comments were printed in this catalog, nor in the minutes of the regent's sessions, nor in the local newspaper. During this year eight women actually attended classes.

5. Mary McLean Olney, *Oakland, Berkeley, and the University of California*, oral history interview conducted by Willa Baum (Regional Oral History Office, Bancroft Library, University of California, Berkeley, 1963), 130–39.

6. In 1870 there were 210,768 women in California and 349,379 men.

7. Elizabeth Griego, "A Study of Women Faculty Members in California in the Late Nineteenth Century" (paper delivered at the History of Education Conference, Stanford University, Palo Alto, California, October 1986).

8. Patricia Graham, "The Cult of True Womanhood: Past and Present," in *All of Us Are Present: The Stephens College Symposium. Women's Education: The Future*, Eleanor Bender, Bobbie Burk, Nancy Walker, eds. (Columbia, Missouri: James Madison Wood Research Institute, 1984), 9–32. See also Barbara Welter, "The Cult of True Womanhood: 1820–1860," in *Women's Experience in America*, Esther Katz and Anita Rapone, eds. (New Brunswick, N.J.: Transaction Books, 1980), 193–218.

9. Geraldine Jonçich Clifford, " 'Shaking Dangerous Questions from the Crease': Gender and Higher Education," *Feminist Issues* 3, no. 2 (fall 1983): 3–62.

10. Maresi Nerad, "The Situation of Women at Berkeley Between 1870 and 1915," in *Feminist Issues*, 7, no. 1 (spring 1987): 67–80. Frederick Rudolph, *Curriculum* (San Francisco: Jossey Bass Publishers, 1977), 138.

11. See also Lynn Gordon, "Women at the University of California 1870–1920: From Pelicans to Chickens," in *Gender and Education in the Progressive Era* (New Haven: Yale University Press, 1990), 52–84.

12. Verne A. Stadtman, *The University of California, 1868–1968: A Centennial Publication of the University of California* (San Francisco: McGraw-Hill, 1970).

13. *The Biennial Report of the President of the University, 1900–1902* (University of California Archives, Bancroft Library, University of California, Berkeley), (hereafter *President's Report* followed by years of publication) 21.

14. She was the eleventh person to receive a doctorate at the university. Her doctoral thesis, "The Sensory Development of Infants with Pedagogical Applications," gained attention from psychologists and educated people generally in the United States and abroad. For some years her work was among the few systematic observations of infants available in English. She was also an editor and regular contributor of both poetry and prose to the *Overland Monthly*, an intellectual journal of the Pacific Coast.

15. *President's Report, 1900–1902*, 63.

16. Ibid.

17. Patricia A. Graham, "Expansion and Exclusion: A History of Women in American Higher Education," *Signs* 3, no. 4 (1978): 766.

18. When Stanford opened in 1891, one-third of the students were women. In 1895, for every 100 men there were 51 women. With this rapid increase, together with a series of athletic losses by Stanford's male students to Berkeley, the argument was made that men students turned to "queening" rather than to hard athletic practice. When in 1899 women were 40 percent of the total registration, Mrs. Stanford limited the number of women students at any one time to 500 so that Stanford would not become a Vassar of the West Coast. This quota was eliminated during the depression in 1933 when the university badly needed student fees. See Orrin Leslie Elliott, *Stanford University: The First Twenty-Five Years* (Stanford: Stanford University Press, 1937), 133.

19. *President's Report, 1910–1912*, 5.

20. Although these educators varied in some degree in their views on women's higher education and the question of coeducation, they shared common assumptions about the "naturalness" of women's behavior.

21. Sari Knopp Biklen, "The Progressive Education Movement and the Question of Women," *Teachers College Record*, 80 (December 1978): 307–15.

22. This all-women student government was established in 1894. Although Wheeler came to Berkeley as president in 1899, it took him five years to recognize the women students' organization.

23. *Daily Californian*, 1 September 1904: 1.

24. Charles W. Eliot, "Women's Education, a Forecast," speech presented at the twenty-sixth annual meeting of the Association of College Alumnae, Boston, November 1907; printed in *Association of Collegiate Alumnae Magazine*, 3rd series, no. 17, (February 1908): 105.

25. *Daily Californian*, 27 February 1905: 1.

26. Verne Stadtman, *The University of California, 1868–1968* (New York: McGraw Hill, 1970); Laurence Veysey, *The Emergence of the American University* (Chicago: The University of Chicago Press, 1965).

27. Monroe E. Deutsch, ed., *The Abundant Life* (Berkeley: University of California Press, 1926), 6.

28. Michael Otten, *University Authority and the Student* (Berkeley: University of California Press, 1970).

29. After Alice Freeman Palmer, president of Wellesley from 1881 through 1987 and dean of women at the University of Chicago from 1892, died unexpectedly, Lucy Sprague, who was a close family friend, took care of the widower.

30. Lucy Sprague Mitchell, *Pioneering in Education*, oral history interview conducted by Irene Prescott, Regional Oral History Office, Bancroft Library, University of California, Berkeley, 1962), 61.

31. Agnes Fay Morgan, *Oral History*, oral history interview conducted by Alexander Callow (Centennial History of the University of California project, Regional Oral History Office, Bancroft Library, University of California, Berkeley, 1959).

32. Ibid., 23.

33. Stadtman, *University of California*, 192–193.

34. Helen R. Olin, *The Women of a State University* (New York: G. P. Putnam's Sons, The Knickerbocker Press, 1909), 110.

35. Mitchell, *Pioneering in Education*, 62.

36. We know nothing about Mrs. Wheeler's opinion of women's higher education, nor are there any writings by Benjamin Wheeler on women's higher education or on home economics as an academic subject in general. Unfortunately, all of Wheeler's personal papers were lost during the 1923 Berkeley fire.

37. Charles Van Hise, "Education Tendencies in State Universities," an address given before the Association of Collegiate Alumnae at the quarter-centennial meeting in Boston, 6 November 1907, printed in *Educational Review* 34 (1907): 504–20. The author himself stated that "the discussion was not prepared with particular reference to the University of Wisconsin, but was a general consideration of coeducation, based upon facts and opinions furnished me by the presidents of nearly all the state universities of the country." Helen R. Olin, *The Women of a State University* (New York: G. P. Putnam's Sons, The Knickerbocker Press, 1909), 110.

38. Van Hise, "Education Tendencies in State Universities," 511.

39. Ibid., 517.

40. As mentioned earlier, Stanford limited women's enrollment to 500. Wesleyan set a 20 percent quota on women students.

41. *President's Report, 1900–1902*, 13. The Hearst Domestic Industries was established by Regent Phoebe Hearst to provide an income for women students who taught children in the Berkeley slum area to sew, cook, sweep, and clean.

42. See the section on summer sessions in *President's Reports, 1904–1906, 1906–1908, 1908–1910*.

43. Bevier, *Home Economics*.

44. Marion Talbot and Lois Kimball Mathews Rosenberry, *The History of the America Association of University Women, 1881–1931* (Boston: The Riverside Press, Cambridge, 1931), 198.

45. Mary Gibson, ed., *A Record of Twenty-Five Years of California Federation of Women's Clubs, 1900–1925*, vol. 1 (The California Federation of Women's Clubs, 1927), 225, 234–35.

46. *The Daily Californian*, 12 March 1909: 1.

47. Among the members of the Town and Gown club was President Wheeler's wife. Peixotto was a member of the San Francisco branch of the ACA and was very active in the San Francisco City federation of the women's clubs.

48. Mary Bennett Ritter, *More Than Gold in California* (Berkeley: University of California Press, 1933).

49. "Dean of Women Report," *President's Report, 1910–1912*, 56.

50. It is likely that Peixotto was familiar with the ideas of Charlotte Perkins Gilman who proposed to socialize housework. (For example, the preparation of meals would be done by paid workers, male and female, in communal kitchens.) Gilman lived in San Francisco from 1894 through 1900.

51. Henry Rand Hatfield, "Jessica Blanche Peixotto," in *Essays in Social Economics: In Honor of Jessica Blanche Peixotto* (Berkeley: University of California Press, 1935), 5–14.

52. Ibid., 6.

53. Phoebe Hearst, a Missouri school teacher before her marriage to millionaire Senator George Hearst, donated much of her time and money

to the university and its women students. After the death of her husband in 1891, she donated annual tuition scholarships for needy undergraduate women. She also donated to the European scholarship fund for graduate women's research abroad. From 1897 to 1919 Phoebe Hearst served as the first and only woman member of the university's board of regents.

54. Jessica Peixotto to Millicent Shinn, 12 July 1846 (U.C. Archives).

55. Mary E. Cookingham, "Social Economics and Modern Reform: Berkeley, 1906–1961," *History of Political Economy* 19, no. 1 (spring 1987): 47–65.

56. Jessica Peixotto to President Wheeler, 15 January 1913 (U.C. Archives).

57. See Ellen Fitzpatrick, *Endless Crusade: Women Social Scientists and Progressive Reform* (New York: Oxford University Press, 1990); Kathleen D. McCarthy, ed., *Lady Bountiful Revisited: Women, Philanthropy, and Power* (New Brunswick, N.J.; London: Rutgers University Press, 1990); Robyn Muncy, *Creating a Female Dominion in American Reform, 1890–1935* (New York: Oxford University Press, 1991).

58. Ella Barrows Hagar, *Continuing Memoirs: Family, Community, University*, oral history interview conducted by Suzanne Riess (Regional Oral History Office, Bancroft Library, University of California, Berkeley, 1973).

59. *The Women's Faculty Club of the University of California, Berkeley, 1919–1982.* (Oral History Project, Regional Oral History Office, Bancroft Library, University of California, Berkeley, 1983): 44.

60. Ira Brown Cross, *Portrait of an Economics Professor*, oral history interview conducted by Joan Dietz Ariff (Regional Oral History Office, Bancroft Library, University of California, Berkeley, 1967).

61. Lucy Sprague Mitchell, *Pioneering in Education*, oral history interview conducted by Irene Prescott (Regional Oral History Office, Bancroft Library, University of California, Berkeley, 1961): 31.

62. Peixotto to Wheeler, 14 March 1917 (U.C. Archives).

63. Hatfield, "Peixotto," 14.

64. Joyce Antler, "Mitchell, Lucy Sprague," in *Notable American Women: The Modern Period*, Barbara Sicherman and Carol Hurd Green, eds. (Cambridge, Mass: The Belknapp Press, 1980), 484–87.

65. Joyce Antler, Lucy Sprague Mitchell: *The Making of a Modern Woman* (New Haven: Yale University Press, 1987), 47.

66. Lucy Sprague Mitchell, *Two Lives: The Story of Wesley Clair Mitchell and Myself* (New York: Simon and Schuster, 1953), 194.

67. "Dean of Women Report," *President's Report, 1904–1905*, 106–07.

68. Mitchell, *Oral History*, 41.

69. Antler, "Mitchell," 486.

70. Mitchell, *Oral History*, 51.

71. Mitchell, *Two Lives*, 196.

72. "Dean of Women Report," *President's Report, 1905–1906*, 109.

73. See William Ferrier, *Origin and Development of the University of California* (Berkeley: University of California Press, 1930)

74. Mary Blossom Davis was assistant dean of women from 1913 through 1941, when she became dean after Lucy Stebbins's retirement and remained in this position until 1951.

75. "Dean of Women Report," *President's Report, 1913–1914*, 196–97.

76. "Dean of Women Report," *President's Report, 1915–1916*.

77. Exceptions were, of course, the physical education and hygiene courses for women.

78. Harold S. Wechsler, "An Academic Gresham's Law: Group Repulsion as a Theme in American Higher Education," *Teachers College Record* 82, no. 4 (summer 1981): 567–88.

79. Rudolph, *Curriculum*, 138. Land-grant colleges and universities are institutions that were founded under the Morrill Act of 1862, which authorized states to select and sell from their public lands 30,000 acres for each member they sent to Congress. The proceeds were to be used for the creation of a perpetual fund. The interest of this fund allowed each state to maintain at least one college or university whose primary purpose was to teach agriculture and the "mechanic arts."

80. Laurence R. Veysey, *The Emergence of the American University* (Chicago: The University of Chicago Press, 1965), 113.

81. Linda Marie Fritschner, "Women's Work and Women's Education: The Case of Home Economics, 1870–1920," *Sociology of Work and Occupations* 4, no. 2 (May 1977): 230.

82. Linda Marie Fritschner, "The Rise and Fall of Home Economics: A Study with Implications for Women, Education, and Change," Ph.D. diss., University of California, Davis, 1973. Technical-functional theory argues

that increased educational offerings are to provide the necessary training for increased job skill demands which result from modernization.

83. Solomon, *In the Company*, 83.

Chapter 2

1. "In Memoriam," *Oakland Tribune*, 5 July 1931.

2. President Wheeler to Meyer Jaffa, 4 August 1909 (U.C. Archives).

3. M. Jaffa to Wheeler, 6 August 1909 (U.C. Archives).

4. Jessica Peixotto to President Wheeler, 29 May 1911 (U.C. Archives).

5. John Galen Howard was the supervising architect under the comprehensive building plan of the university before President Wheeler appointed him to the post of professor in architecture.

6. *Evening Sun*, Baltimore, 27 May 1912.

7. Mary Lois Kissell to President Wheeler, 28 May 1912 (U.C. Archives).

8. Kissell to Wheeler, undated, 1912 (U.C. Archives).

9. *The Daily Californian*, 12 October 1912.

10. Kissell to Wheeler, 25 November 1912 (U.C. Archives).

11. Kissell to Wheeler, 24 April 1913 (U.C. Archives).

12. In her letters to David Barrows, who administered the university while Wheeler was absent during the summer of 1913, Kissell gave her opinion about the home economics departments at the following universities: Sophia Newcomb Memorial College; Tulane University, New Orleans; University of Chicago; University of Wisconsin, Madison; University of Illinois, Champaign-Urbana; Downer College, Milwaukee.

13. Dr. A. L. Daniels, Ph.D. in physical chemistry from Yale, at the University of Missouri, Columbia, Mo; Dr. N. E. Goldthwaite, Ph.D. in chemistry from the University of Chicago, at the University of Illinois, Champaign-Urbana.

14. It could be that Berkeley's poor treatment of faculty women was known among academic women around the nation. The information probably had traveled through the channels of the Association of the Collegiate Alumnae.

15. Kissell to Wheeler, 25 May 1913 (U.C. Archives).

16. M. Jaffa to Wheeler, 10 April 1913 (U.C. Archives).

17. M. Jaffa to Wheeler, 6 August 1909, when Jaffa was appointed to join the Committee on Domestic Science (U.C. Archives).

18. Barrows to Kissell, 2 July 1913 (U.C. Archives).

19. See *University Course Catalogue, 1913–1914* (U.C. Archives), 26.

20. Kissell to Barrows 18 July 1913 (U.C. Archives).

21. Dr. Adelle Jaffa to Wheeler, 23 January 1914 (U.C. Archives).

22. *University Course Catalogue, 1913–1914*, 26.

23. Wheeler to A. Jaffa, 10 February 1914 (U.C. Archives).

24. Kissell to Wheeler, 15 January 1914 (U.C. Archives).

25. Ibid.

26. Wheeler to Peixotto, 19 January 1914 (U.C. Archives).

27. Kissell to Wheeler, 26 December 1913 (U.C. Archives).

28. Report from the secretary of the Home Economics Committee (formerly Domestic Science Committee) to President Wheeler, 10 April 1913 (President's files, U.C. Archives).

29. Kissell to Wheeler, 15 January 1914 (U.C. Archives).

30. Ibid.

31. Wheeler to Dean Thomas F. Hunt, College of Agriculture, 3 February 1914 (U.C. Archives).

32. Wheeler to Kissell, 3 February 1914 (U.C. Archives).

33. Report of the Committee on Home Economics to Wheeler, 4 March 1914 (President's files, U.C. Archives).

34. This is from a 1914 draft entitled "Some Propositions relating to the Status, Needs, Organization and Administration of 'Home Economics' in the University of California." Presumably this draft was written by Peixotto, chair of the committee; she was probably asked to draft a working paper for the committee.

35. Wheeler to Barrows, 9 March 1914 (U.C. Archives).

36. Ibid.

37. *The Daily Californian*, 7 February 1922, 6.

38. Barrows to Richard Boone, 3 April 1914 (U.C. Archives).

39. Boone to Barrows, 14 April 1914 (U.C. Archives).

40. Memorandum, Secretary Maxwell, 9 September 1914 (U.C. Archives).

41. The Regents' Minutes, 18, 8 December 1914, 143.

42. Ibid., 18, 11 August 1914, 178.

43. It was not unusual for a middle-class woman at this time to start higher education in her thirties, after fulfilling traditional family expectations of an education in the fine arts, housework, and sewing. Peixotto started her studies at Berkeley when she was approaching her thirties.

44. Mary Patterson to Wheeler, 24 December 1915 (U.C. Archives).

45. Wheeler to Patterson, 27 December 1915 (U.C. Archives).

46. The original letter from Wheeler to the committee could not be found. However, the answering letter of the committee quoted Wheeler's proposal. Letter from Lucy Ward Stebbins, secretary, Study-Lists Committee on Home Economics to President Wheeler, 16 February 1916 (U.C. Archives).

47. Ibid.

48. Ibid.

49. Ibid.

50. Wheeler to the Committee on Home Economics, 14 April 1916 (U.C. Archives).

51. Ibid.

52. Regents' Minutes, 19, 11 April 1916, 66.

53. *University of California, Courses of Instruction, 1916–17*, 148.

54. I have analyzed this case by applying the implementation analysis approach to it. According to this approach, we would have an instance of successful implementation. Our example shows that if we compare the original goals with the observed outcomes we will discover that the implementation approach inherently has a top-down view. Analysis according to logical, content adequate criteria, was a failed implementation.

CHAPTER 3

1. Morgan, *Oral History*, 4.

2. I. D. Raacke, "Agnes Fay Morgan," *Notable American Women: The Modern Period*, Barbara Sicherman et al., eds. (Cambridge: The Belknap Press of Harvard, 1980), 495.

3. Rosalind Rosenberg, *Beyond Separate Spheres* (New Haven: Yale University Press, 1982).

4. Marie Dye, *History of Home Economics, University of Chicago* (Chicago: Home Economics Alumni Association, 1972), 343–50.

5. Morgan, *Oral History*, 3.

6. Margaret W. Rossiter, *Women Scientists in America, Struggles and Strategies to 1940* (Baltimore: Johns Hopkins University Press, 1981), 161.

7. Stieglitz, also married to a practicing chemist—Mary Rising—encouraged and supported many of his able women students. Agnes Fay Morgan kept a picture of the stone bust of Professor Stieglitz in her personal files.

8. The statistical data on women scientists are scant and exist only in aggregate form or by decades. See Rossiter, *Struggles and Strategies*; Patricia Graham, "Expansion and Exclusion: A History of Women in American," *Signs* 3, no. 4 (Summer 1978): 766.

9. Rossiter, *Struggles and Strategies*, 131.

10. Rossiter critically discussed early surveys of women faculty and came to the conclusion that 75 percent of the women were instructors. (See Rossiter, *Struggles and Strategies*, 110.) The only figures on faculty marriage rates are from 1920 and include all professional women. Twenty percent of all employed professional women were married. William Chafe, *The American Woman: Her Changing Social, Economic, and Political Role, 1920–1970* (New York: Oxford University Press, 1972), 100.

11. Rossiter, *Struggles and Strategies*, 195. See also Jessie Bernard, *Academic Women* (University Park: The Pennsylvania State University Press, 1964), 40, table 2.2.

12. On this issue, see also Geraldine J. Clifford, ed., *Lone Voyagers: Academic Women in Coeducational American Universities* (New York: Feminist Press, 1989), 30–31.

13. See Regents' Minutes, 18, 1914–1915 (U.C. Archives).

14. *Women's Faculty Club*, Oral History.

15. Agnes Fay Morgan, "Closing Remarks," *Landmarks of a Half a Century of Nutrition Research: A Symposium Honoring Dr. Agnes Fay Morgan's Fiftieth Anniversary at the University of California, Berkeley, May 8, 1965* reprinted in *The Journal of Nutrition*, supp. 1, part 2, 91, (February 1967): 66.

16. Lillian Morgan, interview by author, October 1987.

17. Ruth Okey, "Agnes Fay Morgan (1884–1968)—A Biographical Sketch," *The Journal of Nutrition* 104, no.9, (September 1974): 1106. This behavior has been confirmed in several of my personal interviews with former students of Morgan. Since anonymity was promised in these interviews, no names are used here, only the dates of the interviews.

18. For example, Isabel Bevier, head of the Department of Home Economics at the University of Illinois, during an interview in 1929, insisted that she was not a feminist. See Rossiter, *Struggles and Strategies*, 355 n.44.

19. Rossiter, *Struggles and Strategies*, 121.

20. Agnes Fay Morgan, ed., *A History of Iota Sigma Pi* (University Archives, Bancroft Library, University of California, Berkeley, 1963).

21. For more details, see Rossiter, *Struggles and Strategies*, 297–312.

22. Ibid., 297.

23. Among the founding members were Lucy Ward Stebbins, Jessica Peixotto, Pauline Sperry (professor of mathematics), Alice Tabor (lecturer in the German department), Margaret Beattie (professor in bacteriology), and Barbara Armstrong (law). *Women's Faculty Club*, Oral History, 30.

24. Later, its membership also included women on the administrative staff, such as administrative assistants and secretaries of the president, deans, or department chairs.

25. Today, it still serves these functions. In fact, the Berkeley Women's Faculty Club is most often a preferred place for visitors and social events over the Faculty Club.

26. For example, Lucy Sprague, Marion Talbot, and Alice Norton.

27. The fact that Agnes Fay Morgan was not a student of the famous Yale professor in physiological chemistry, Lafayette B. Mendel, barred her from becoming president of the American Institute of Nutrition. For more details see Rossiter, *Struggles and Strategies*, 278. *Uneasy Careers and*

Intimate Lives, Women in Science 1789–1979, Pnina G. Abir-Am and Dorinda Outram, eds., (New Brunswick: Rutgers University Press, 1987), illuminates and analyzes commonalities and differences in the work and lives of women scientists.

28. This was another strategy to which women scientists were forced if they wanted to stay in the field, as Pnina Abir-Am and Dorinda Outram showed in *Uneasy Careers.*

29. Okey, "Morgan," 1106. Several of Morgan's former students also commented on this fact.

30. Raacke, "Morgan," 496.

31. John Bennett, *Managing the Academic Department: Cases and Notes* (New York: American Council on Education, Macmillan Publishing Company, 1983).

32. Cary Cherniss, "New Settings in the University: Their Creation, Problems, and Early Development," Ph.D. diss., Yale University, 1972, 219.

33. Ibid., 221. Cherniss did not think at all in terms of gender. If he had done so, his explanations of the differences in history among the four departments would have been more complete. In only one sentence did he acknowledge the fact that gender might also have something to do with marginality: "In addition, certain groups of people, such as women and 'special students,' were perceived by the academic community as socially marginal" (205). But he failed to integrate this fact into his final analysis. I am not arguing that gender was the sole criterion, but it is one among others.

34. Morgan, *Oral History,* 5–6.

35. Ibid., 7–8.

36. L. W. Stebbins to the Advisory Council of Deans, 10 May 1918 (U.C. Archives).

37. Okey, "Morgan," 1103.

38. A. F. Morgan to President Barrows, 27 April 1920 (U.C. Archives).

39. G. Lauderbach to Dean of the Faculties, John Merriam, 17 June 1920 (U.C. Archives).

40. The Department of Household Art existed until 1939. Thereafter it changed its name to the Department of Decorative Art, and in 1964, it was transferred from the College of Letters and Science into the College of Environmental Design and became the Department of Design.

41. With the United States entering World War I in 1917, Wheeler was accused of pro-German sentiments, especially since he had been an invited guest at the court of the German Kaiser at Berlin in 1909 and 1913. In addition, the faculty rebelled against his paternalistic and autocratic style. Stadtman, *University of California*, 201.

42. O. Templin, U.S. Food Administration, to A. F. Morgan, 4 May 1918 (U.C. Archives).

43. References to these courses can be found at many places, e.g., Minutes, Committee on Courses of Instruction, February 1918; the *University Chronicle*, 1918; Agnes Fay Morgan, "The History of Nutrition and Home Economics in the University of California, Berkeley, 1914–1962" (U.C. Archives), 8.

44. *President's Report, 1918–1919*, 27.

45. See also Rossiter, *Struggles and Strategies*, on women and the war, 119–22.

46. *President's Report, 1918*, 12. Also see page 13 for further description of Berkeley's faculty wartime service.

47. "Dean of Women Report," *President's Report, 1917–1918*, 184.

48. Estelle Freedman, "Separatism as Strategy: Female Institution Building and American Feminism, 1870–1930," *Feminist Studies*, 5, no. 3 (fall 1979): 512–29.

49. Freedman developed Michelle Zimbalist Rosaldo's argument about "women's societies and African queens" into a thesis about political strategies for women. Michelle Zimbalist Rosaldo and Louise Lamphere, eds., *Women, Culture, and Society* (Stanford: Stanford University Press, 1974).

50. Chapter 6 will elaborate on this point.

51. Okey, "Agnes Fay Morgan," 1106.

52. Hutchison, *Oral History*, 323.

53. Okey, "Morgan," 1106.

54. Ruth Okey, Barbara Kennedy Johnson, Gordon Mackinney, "Agnes Fay Morgan, 1884–1968," *In Memoriam* (Berkeley: University of California, May 1969), 79.

CHAPTER 4

1. Rossiter, *Struggles and Strategies*, 67.

2. For more information see Dye, *History of Home Economics*; Rossiter, *Struggles and Strategies*, 201.

3. Okey et al., *In Memoriam*, 79.

4. Martin Trow, "Analysis of Status," in Burton Clark, ed., *Perspectives on Higher Education: Eight Disciplinary and Comparative Views* (Berkeley: University of California Press, 1984), 132–64; also Martin Trow "The American Academic Department as a Context for Learning," *Studies in Higher Education* 1, no. 1 (March 1976): 11–22.

5. Icie Gertrude Macy Hoobler, *Boundless Horizons: Portrait of a Pioneer Woman Scientist* (New York: Exposition Press, 1982).

6. From 1940 to 1954 only lecturers and associates did not have Ph.D.s. These were titles often given to graduate students.

7. I concur with Margaret Rossiter that more work needs to be done on the relationship between these women pioneers who according to Rossiter were given the nickname "the generals of women's work." Rossiter, *Struggles and Strategies*, 203.

8. Okey, "Morgan," 1103.

9. Morgan, *Oral History*, 21–22.

10. Ibid., 11.

11. Agnes Fay Morgan, "High School Courses in Science of the Household, Nutrition, and Citizen-Homemaking," *The School Review*, 1, no. 24 (May 1927): 521; A. F. Morgan, "Home Economics Courses and the Higher Institutions of Learning," *The School Review* 28, no. 7 (September 1920); A. F. Morgan, "Let's Consider Home Economics," *Omicron Nu* 3, no. 40 (winter 1947).

12. Agnes Fay Morgan, "A New Look for the Old-Fashioned Liberal Education of Women," *American Association of University Professors Bulletin* 39, no. 2 (summer 1953): 261–62.

13. Agnes Fay Morgan, "Professional Training the Major Concern," *The Journal of Home Economics* 43, no. 4 (April 1951): 253–56.

14. *The Iotan Newsletter*, no. 34 (November 1983); *Nutrition Research* 22, no. 1 (October 1968); *The Journal of Nutrition*, supp. part 2, 91, no. 2 (February 1967).

15. Okey et al., *In Memoriam*.

16. Monroe Deutsch, Provost of the Faculty, to Morgan, 22 March 1937 (U.C. Archives).

17. I participated in the fortieth anniversary of the home economics class of 1945 held at Berkeley in May 1985.

18. The various engineering programs at Berkeley did not have a particularly low status.

19. Doris Howes Calloway, "21st Lenna Frances Cooper Memorial Lecture: Nutrition Research by and about Women," *Journal of the American Dietetic Association* 84, no. 6 (June 1984): 642.

20. Ibid.

21. Ibid., 644, 647.

22. Morgan, *Oral History*, 9.

23. See more details on Morgan's research in her curriculum vitae; Okey, "Morgan"; Okey et al., *In Memoriam; The Faculty Bulletin of the University of California*, 1950, 41–42; Edna Southmayd, "Careers in Nutrition," *Nutrition Research* 22, no. 1 (October 1968): 1–4.

24. Rossiter, *Struggles and Strategies*, 288.

25. Gladys A. Emerson, "Agnes Fay Morgan and Early Nutrition Discoveries in California," paper presented at the sixtieth Annual Meeting of the Federation of American Societies for Experimental Biology, Anaheim, California, 12 April 1976.

26. Okey, "Morgan," 1105.

27. Ruth Okey, "Experiences of a Woman Trained in Science in the Years Preceding the Formation of the Present Department of Nutritional Sciences at U.C. Berkeley," Nutritional Sciences Library, University of California, 1981, 11.

28. Emerson, *Agnes Fay Morgan*, 2.

29. Okey, "Experiences," 14.

30. Morgan, "Closing Remarks," 65.

31. A. Leuschner to Provost Deutsch, 10 October 1934 (U.C. Archives).

32. Rossiter, *Struggles and Strategies*, 200.

33. Okey, "A Woman in Science: 1893–1973," *Journal of Nutrition* 118 (1988): 1425–31.

34. Charles Lipman to A. F. Morgan, 27 August 1924 (U.C. Archives).

35. Report on proposed candidacy of Miss Statie E. Erikson for the Ph.D. degree, 4 September 1924 (U.C. Archives).

36. A. F. Morgan to Dean Lipman, 8 September 1924 (U.C. Archives).

37. Dean Lipman to G. Anderson, 3 December 1930 (U.C. Archives).

38. A. F. Morgan to Dean Lipman, 15 December 1930 (U.C. Archives).

39. Ibid.

40. A. F. Morgan to Dean Lipman, 20 December 1930 (U.C. Archives).

41. Dean Lipman to A. F. Morgan, 26 January 1931 (U.C. Archives).

42. A. F. Morgan to Dean Lipman, 31 October 1932 (U.C. Archives).

43. Morgan, "Closing Remarks," 66; G. Emerson, *Agnes Fay Morgan*, 7; Okey, "Morgan," 1104; a list of all the names, dissertation titles, and years of degrees awarded is attached to the "History of Nutrition and Home Economics at the University of California, Berkeley, 1914–1962" (U.C. Archives) written by A. F. Morgan.

44. Okey, "Experiences," 8.

45. *San Francisco Chronicle*, 19 October 1926.

46. Okey, "Experiences," 16.

47. Ibid., 19.

48. Agnes Fay Morgan, "History of Nutrition," 4.

49. Clark Kerr, interview by the author, 6 March 1985.

50. Morgan, *Oral History*, 47. Obviously, she did not show solidarity with the education department, another traditional female field with low status.

51. One of the male administrators interviewed by the author, when asked to describe Dr. Morgan, told a story in which others referred to her as a "bitch."

52. Clark Kerr, interviewed by the author, 6 March 1985.

53. "Annual Report of Household Science," *President's Report, 1936* (U.C. Archives), 7.

54. The Garvan Medal was established in 1935 by Francis P. Garvan as an award for a distinguished *woman* chemist. Without this specific compensatory award for women, none of the contributions made by women in

chemistry would have been publicized at all. See Rossiter, *Struggles and Strategies*, 308–12, for more detail.

55. Historical Statement, The Annual Faculty Research Lecturer, Academic Senate.

56. *Women's Faculty Club*, Oral History, 4.

57. The State of California required faculty, who were employees of the state, to take an oath testifying that they were not members of the Communist party. To protest this state policy, several famous faculty members left the university.

58. Hutchison, *Oral History*, 316–17.

59. E. D. Merrill to President Campbell, 31 January 1924.

60. President Campbell to Dr. Morgan, 4 February 1924.

61. Ibid., 4 March 1924.

62. Dr. Morgan claimed that Schmidt envied her for being advanced to full professorship ahead of him. "As soon as he heard about my professorship he became incensed and went to see David Barrows and had a long controversy with him about it, and the next year he got his professorship." Morgan, *Oral History*, 50.

63. R. Clausen to Professor Peterson, 11 April 1924.

64. Speech read before the joint meeting of Experiment Station and Home Economics Research Sections of the Agriculture and Home Economics Divisions of the Association of the Land-Grant Colleges and Universities, Washington, D.C., 8 November 1948, 1.

65. Morgan, "A New Look for the Old-Fashioned Liberal Education of Women," *American Association of University Professors Bulletin* 39, no. 2 (Summer 1953): 263.

66. G. Briggs to Chancellor E. Strong, 6 October 1961.

67. G. Briggs to Dean E. Linsley, 9 January 1961.

68. Morgan, "Closing Remarks," 68.

69. Rossiter, *Struggles and Strategies*, xvi.

70. Arlie Hochschild, "Making It: Marginality and Obstacles to Minority Consciousness," *Annals of the New York Academy of Sciences* 208 (March 1973): 183.

CHAPTER 5

1. President Robert G. Sproul, 14 July 1954 (President's files, U.C. Archives).

2. In "Minority Set of Recommendations for Berkeley," the Davis Educational Policy Committee unanimously urged "that Home Economics continue on the four campuses where it is now established." Committee on Educational Policy, Report of Higher Education, 30 June 1955.

3. Jessie Coles to Vice President for Agricultural Sciences Harry R. Wellman, 7 November 1955 (Chancellor's files, U.C. Archives).

4. Wellman to Coles, 8 November 1955 (Chancellor's files, U.C. Archives).

5. Knowles A. Ryerson, *The World Is My Campus*, interviewed by Joann Larkey. (Oral History Shields Library, University of California, Davis, 1977) 324–25.

6. Ibid, 325.

7. Committee on Educational Policy, "Report on Home Economics," 20 June 1955 (Chancellor's files, U.C. Archives).

8. Committee on Educational Policy, "Report on Home Economics," 30 June 1955 (President's files, U.C. Archives). This report was sent to Sproul by the committee chairman, Robert E. Connick, on 6 July 1955.

9. David Gardener, *The California Oath Controversy* (Berkeley: University of California Press, 1967).

10. Stadtman, *University of California*.

11. Author interview with Clark Kerr, 6 March 1985.

12. See Paula Fass, *Outside In: Minorities and the Transformation of American Education* (New York: Oxford University Press, 1989), chapter 5.

13. Hutchison, *Oral History*, 314.

14. Wellman at the Academic Advisory Committee meeting on 5 November 1955. Minutes of the meeting (Chancellor's files, U.C. Archives).

15. *A Restudy of the Needs of California in Higher Education*, prepared by the Liaison Committee of the Regents of the University of California and the California State Board of Education (Sacramento: California State Department of Education, 1955).

16. T. R. McConnell was formerly chancellor of the University of Buffalo.

17. *Restudy*, 151.

18. Ibid., 218.

19. Committee on Educational Policy, "Report on Home Economics," 30 June 1955.

20. Minutes of the Chancellor's Academic Advisory Committee, 11 April 1956.

21. Ibid., 2.

22. Margaret W. Rossiter, *Women Scientists in America, Before Affirmative Action* (Baltimore: Johns Hopkins University Press, 1995), 166.

23. Author interview with Angela Little, 17 May 1985.

24. Dye, *History of Home Economics*.

25. Rossiter, *Before Affirmative Action*, 180.

26. Ibid., 180.

27. Ibid., 182.

28. Ibid., 183.

29. Ibid., 181.

Conclusion

1. See also Rossiter, *Before Affirmative Action*, 165.

2. Author interview with Clark Kerr, 6 March 1985. Rossiter found that central administrators who held hostile attitudes toward home economics admitted unabashed ignorance about what the field was and what it was trying to do. Rossiter, *Before Affirmative Action*, 164.

3. Maresi Nerad, "Doctoral Education at the University of California and Factors Affecting Time to Degree," a report prepared for the Office of the President, University of California, June 1991.

BIBLIOGRAPHIC ESSAY

METHODOLOGY

Pursuing the history of home economics at Berkeley was at times like piecing together the puzzle of a detective story. To understand the process by which the new field of home economics made its way into the University of California and in order to analyze the university's reaction to a women's department, I combined organizational theory with historiography on the education of women, particularly the higher education of women. This approach merged the classical organizational theory themes and outlooks on power and control, sanctions and rewards, organizational resistance to change, and organizational striving for survival and expansion with the view that women are active forces of change within organizations, that they develop their own ideas and goals, their own informal networks and formal professional organizations, that women occupy both the public domain and the private domain. In particular, I applied and combined gender stratification theory and the analysis of status in higher education to capture the implications of gender for status within a university environment. This combination of several social science theories also allowed me to capture the interaction between the university and its women, both individually and in departmental units.

HISTORY OF HOME ECONOMICS AS AN ACADEMIC FIELD

Until now, no critical history of home economics as an academic field for women has been published. This is astonishing because most colleges, with the exception of the eastern women's colleges, and most coeducational universities have offered home economics from the turn of the century until the late 1950s, or even until today. Books on this subject have been written primarily by home economists. *Home Economics in Higher Education* by the Committee for Evaluating College Programs in Home Economics, Gladys Brannegan, chair, and Ivol Spafford, editor and collaborator (Washington, 1949), commissioned by the American Home Economics Association, is a handbook on how to evaluate undergraduate home economics programs. *Home Economics Past, Present and Future* (Boston: Allyn and Bacon, 1980), by Marjorie East, reviews the history of home economics without considering the development, structure, or changes in higher education nor providing discussion of any external political or economics pressure on the field. It also does not consider the issues of gender, status, power, and prestige. The book reads more like an emphatic defense of home economics than an analytical history of the field. Although Margaret Rossiter noted that a history of the field has still to be written, her two books, *Women Scientists in America: Struggles and Strategies to 1940* (Baltimore: Johns Hopkins University Press, 1982) and *Women Scientists in America: Before Affirmative Action 1940–1972* (Baltimore: Johns Hopkins University Press, 1995), come closest to an analysis of home economics as an academic field. Soon a long-awaited book coedited by feminist historian Sara Stage and home economics scholar Virginia Vincenti, *Rethinking Home Economics* (Cornell: Cornell University Press, 1997), may fill the void.

Several unpublished dissertations from various decades and disciplines concern themselves with home economics as an academic discipline. The quality of these varies greatly, and the role and significance of home economics is interpreted very differently according to whether the author is a historian of education, a sociologist, a home economist, or a feminist.

During the last fifteen years a few books have appeared that touch upon this topic. Most of these studies cover the period between 1870 and 1920 (Lynn Gordon 1990; Geraldine J. Clifford, ed., 1989; Laura Shapiro 1986; Louise Newman, ed., 1985; Barbara

Solomon Miller 1985). After 1920, the topic was abandoned by most historians with the exception of Mabel Newcomer (1956) and Charlotte Conable (1977).

RECONSTRUCTING BERKELEY'S HOME ECONOMICS HISTORY

Reconstructing the history of the Berkeley Department of Home Economics meant piecing together four diverse sources: primary University of California archival sources; statistical data detailing enrollment, degrees, and departmental funds; oral history interviews of former Berkeley students and faculty conducted, transcribed, and edited by the University of California Regional Oral History Office; and twenty-five in-depth interviews conducted with previous university administrators and with faculty and students of the former home economics and the later nutritional sciences department.

The University of California primary archival sources used here included official correspondence of university faculty, administrators, and staff; the Department of Home Economics' files; minutes of campus committees; biennial reports of the presidents; the annual university catalogs; daily student newspapers; alumni and faculty magazines and journals; bibliographical essays written in honor of deceased faculty; the registrar's reports; and the Centennial Record of the University, 1967. Checking the contents of the Department of Home Economics' unindexed files against the contents of the 1916 to 1962 correspondence of the office of the president allowed me to place themes and events that were dealt with in both places in a general campus context. Comparing the correspondence of key players involved in the events of the Department of Home Economics, including that of the deans of women, the chairs of the biochemistry department, Academic Senate Committee members involved in decision-making processes, with the home economics department's files proved to be worthwhile as a method of gaining a more balanced insight into events and plans, since a diversity of perceptions is taken into consideration.

Unexpectedly, for this study the minutes of the University of California Regents' meetings turned out to be disappointing as a source. They contained only passed resolutions and were missing any summary of the discussion. Official university publications, such as the annual or biennial reports of the president, contributed substantially to painting a picture of Berkeley's formal institutional character and image. In particular, the president's biennial reports during the first fifty years of the university contained reports of the dean of women and an extensive statistical addendum on enrollment and degree data.

However, providing consistent statistics on the enrollment of and degrees awarded to women and men proved to be not only a laborious but also a fruitless undertaking. The president's reports presented the figures in a different format each year, and these figures did not match those printed in the registrar's reports. Given these inconsistencies, I used the figures presented in the *Centennial Record of the University*, compiled and edited by Verne Stadtman in 1967.

As a first step in learning the names of newly hired faculty and in learning about the addition and deletion of course offerings in home economics, the university catalogs proved to be useful. *The Daily Californian*, the Berkeley campus daily student newspaper, *Students' Opinion*, a student magazine, and other alumni and faculty magazines and journals helped to illuminate how particular events were perceived by the larger campus community.

Although oral history interviews are not accurate sources to trace a campus history chronologically, these transcribed and edited interviews with high-level campus administrators and faculty undertaken by the Regional Oral History Office of the University of California, Berkeley, served as an excellent source to understand the way in which people are connected with each other and to provide background material on individuals. These oral history interviews convey people's opinions and attitudes toward each other and toward campus events.

Finally, I conducted twenty-five in-depth personal interviews with people involved in some way with the Department of Home Economics. They included professors and former students from the department: Catherine Landreth, Lucille Hurley, Mary Morris, Mary Murai, Lotte Anrich, Helen Ulrich, and Vera Myrak. Faculty of the later Department of Nutritional Sciences included Doris Calloway, George Briggs, Angela Little, Mary Ann Williams, and Ruth Huneman, a professor in the School of Public Health. I also interviewed previous university administrators, such as former Chancellor and President Clark Kerr; Dean of the College of

Letters and Science, Lincoln Constance; Vice President of Agriculture Harry Wellman; Dean of the College of Agriculture Knowles Ryerson; and the person coordinating the California Master Plan for Higher Education, T. R. McConnell. On the University of California, Davis, campus I interviewed Chancellors James Meyer and Emil Myrak, formerly dean of the college of agriculture and chair of the division of food technology. In addition, in 1985 I participated in the fortieth reunion of former home economics graduates held in conjunction with the retirement celebration for George Briggs, the man who succeeded Morgan as chair in 1960. These former students' recollections were incomplete in factual terms, but their stories vividly conveyed the attitudes of their peers outside home economics and those of nonhome economics faculty toward home economics students. Further, the informal discussions I had during this reunion led to new leads for further archival work.

As in most historical studies on women, the records kept at the University of California of women's early institutional contributions were sparse or nonexistent. If records existed, they were not indexed. For example, the university archives had astonishingly few documents (correspondence, photographs, etc.) of Jessica Peixotto, the first woman professor and second woman to earn a Ph.D. at Berkeley, but had retained numerous letters and photographs of her father and brother, who were well-known San Francisco citizens.

After Morgan's death, only half of her university files were retained by the archives, and none of this material was indexed at the time of this research. In comparison, most of the files containing material from other outstanding campus faculty were indexed. Morgan's travel logs from her professional trips to Europe in 1931 and 1936, where she visited all the major research laboratories in England and Germany, were regarded as irrelevant by a former university archivist. Only as a result of the efforts of George Briggs, a great collector of historical material, were these travel logs retained—in boxes under his desk. It was Briggs who granted me access to these materials. All in all, researching the story of home economics at Berkeley exposed some of the mechanisms by which women's achievements are suppressed and, as a result, forgotten by the next generation of women.

SELECTED BIBLIOGRAPHY

Abir-Am, Pnina G., and Dorinda Outram, eds. *Uneasy Careers and Intimate Lives: Women in Science 1789–1979*. New Brunswick: Rutgers University Press, 1987.

Acker, Joan. "Women Stratification: A Review of Recent Literature." *Contemporary Sociology* 9 (January 1980): 25–39.

American Home Economics Association. "The Syllabus of Home Economics." *Journal of Home Economics* 4 (April 1913): 164–66.

Antler, Joyce. *Lucy Sprague Mitchell: The Making of a Modern Woman*. New Haven: Yale University Press, 1987.

Baum, Willa K. *Oral History for the Local Historical Society*. American Association for State and Local History, Nashville, Tennessee, 1969.

Beard, Mary. *Women a Force in History: A Study of Traditions and Realities*. New York: MacMillan, 1946.

Beecher, Catherine E. *A Treatise on Domestic Economy for Young Ladies*. 2d ed. New York: Harper and Brothers, 1845.

Bennett, John. *Managing the Academic Department: Cases and Notes*. New York: American Council on Education, Macmillan Publishing Company, 1983.

The Berkeleyan, 1874–1897.

Bernard, Jessie. *Academic Women*. University Park: The Pennsylvania State University Press, 1964.

Bevier, Isabel. *Home Economics in Education*. 2d ed. Philadelphia: J. B. Lippincott Company, 1928.

Bevier, Isabel, and Susannah Usher. *The Home Economics Movement*. 2d ed. Boston: Whitcomb & Barrows, 1912.

Biklen, Sari Knopp. "The Progressive Education Movement and the Question of Women." *Teachers College Record* 80 (December 1978): 307–15.

179

Blair, Karen J. *The Clubwomen as Feminist*. New York: Holmes and Meier Publishers, 1980.

Bowles, Gloria, and Renate D. Klein, eds. *Theories of Women's Studies*. London: Routledge and Kegan Paul, 1983.

Budewig, F. Caroline. "Origin and Development of the Home Economics Idea." Ph.D. diss., Graduate School, George Peabody College for Teachers, 1957.

Calloway, Doris Howes. "21st Lenna Frances Cooper Memorial Lecture: Nutrition Research by and about Women." *Journal of the American Dietetic Association* 84, no. 6 (June 1984): 642–47.

Cartter, Allan. *An Assessment of Quality in Graduate Education*. Washington, D.C.: American Council on Education, 1966.

Carver, Marie Negrie. "Home Economics in Higher Education: Major Changes in Administrative Structure and Curriculum." Ph.D. diss., University of Arizona, 1979.

Chafe, William. *The American Woman: Her Changing Social, Economic, and Political Role, 1920–1970*. New York: Oxford University Press, 1972.

Cheit, Earl. *The Useful Arts and the Liberal Tradition*. New York: McGraw-Hill Book Company, 1975.

Cherniss, Cary. "New Settings in the University: Their Creation, Problems, and Early Development." Ph.D. diss., Yale University, 1972.

Clapp, Edward. "The Adjustment to Co-education." *The University Chronicle* 12 (1899): 333–45.

Clark, Burton. *The Higher Education System: Academic Organization in Cross-National Perspective*. Berkeley: University of California Press, 1983.

_____. *Perspectives on Higher Education: Eight Disciplinary and Comparative Views*. Berkeley: University of California Press, 1984.

Clifford, Geraldine J. "'Shaking Dangerous Questions from the Crease': Gender and American Higher Education." *Feminist Issues* 3, no.2 (fall 1983): 3–62.

_____, ed. *Lone Voyagers: Academic Women in Coeducational American Universities*. New York: Feminist Press, 1988.

Conable, Charlotte W. *Women at Cornell: The Myth of Equal Education*. Ithaca: Cornell University Press, 1977.

The Daily Californian, 1897–1954.

"Dean of Women Report." In *Report of the President, 1904–1920*. University of California Archives, Bancroft Library, University of California, Berkeley.

Dye, Marie. *History of the Department of Home Economics, University of Chicago*. Chicago: Home Economics Alumni Association, 1972.

Elliott, Orrin Leslie. *Stanford University: The First Twenty-Five Years*. Stanford: Stanford University Press, 1937.

Emerson, Gladys A. "Agnes Fay Morgan and Early Nutrition Discoveries in California." Paper presented at the 60th Annual Meeting of the Federation of American Societies for Experimental Biology, Anaheim, Ca., April 12, 1976.

Essays in Social Economics: In Honor of Jessica Blanch Peixotto. Berkeley: University of California Press, 1935.

Evening Sun. Baltimore, May 27, 1912.

The Faculty Bulletin of the University of California, 1950.

Fass, Paula. *Outside In: Minorities and the Transformation of American Education.* New York: Oxford University Press, 1989.

Feldman, Saul. *Escape from the Doll's House: Women in Graduate and Professional School Education.* New York: McGraw-Hill Book Company, 1974.

Ferrier, William. *Origin and Development of the University of California.* Berkeley, 1930.

Fitzpatrick, Ellen. *Endless Crusade: Women Social Scientists and Progressive Reform.* New York: Oxford University Press, 1990.

_____. "Marion Talbot and the University of Chicago." In *Lone Voyagers: Academic Women in American Coeducational Universities, 1869–1937,* Geraldine Clifford, ed. New York: The Feminist Press, 1989.

Frederick, Rudolph. *Curriculum.* San Francisco: Jossey-Bass Publishers, 1977.

Freedman, Estelle. "Separatism as Strategy: Female Institution Building and American Feminism, 1870–1930." *Feminist Studies* 5, no. 3 (fall 1979): 512–29.

Fritschner, Linda Marie. "The Rise and Fall of Home Economics: A Study with Implications for Women, Education, and Change." Ph.D. diss., University of California, Davis, 1973.

_____. "Women's Work and Women's Education: The Case of Home Economics, 1870–1920." *Sociology of Work and Occupations* 4, no. 2 (May 1977): 209–31.

Furniss, Todd, and Patricia Graham, eds. *Women in Higher Education.* Washington, D.C.: American Council on Education, 1972.

Gibson, Mary, ed. *A Record of Twenty-Five Years of California Federation of Women's Clubs, 1900–1925.* Vol. 1. The California Federation of Women's Clubs, 1927.

Gordon, Lynn. "Coeducation on Two Campuses: Berkeley and Chicago, 1890–1912." In *Woman's Being, Woman's Place: Female Identity and Vocation in American History,* Mary Kelley, ed. Boston: G. K. Hall, 1979.

_____. *Gender and Higher Education in the Progressive Era.* New Haven: Yale University Press, 1990.

_____. "Women with Missions: Varieties of College Life in the Progressive Era." Ph.D. diss., University of Chicago, 1980.

Graham, Patricia A. "The Cult of True Womanhood: Past and Present." in

All of Us Are Present: The Stephens College Symposium. Women's Education: The Future, Eleanor Bender, Bobbie Burk, and Nancy Walker, eds. Columbia: James Madison Wood Research Institute, 1984.

_____. "Expansion and Exclusion: A History of Women in American Higher Education." *Signs* 3 (summer 1978): 759–73.

Griego, Elizabeth. "A Part and Yet Apart: Clelia Duel Mosher and Professional Women at the Turn-of-the-Century." Ph.D., diss., University of California, Berkeley, 1983.

_____. "A Study of Women Faculty Members in California in the Late Nineteenth Century." Paper read at the History of Education Society annual meeting, Stanford University, October 1986.

Hartmann, Heidi. "Capitalism, Patriarchy and Job Segregation by Sex." *Signs* 1, no. 1 (spring 1976): 137–70.

Hochschild, Arlie. "Making It: Marginality and Obstacles to Minority Consciousness." *Annals of the New York Academy of Sciences* 208 (March 1973): 179–84.

Hoobler, Icie Gertrude Macy. *Boundless Horizons: Portrait of a Pioneer Woman Scientist.* New York: Exposition Press, 1982.

Hutchison, Claude. Oral history interview conducted by Willa Baum. Regional Oral History Office, Bancroft Library, University of California, Berkeley, 1962.

The Iotan Newsletter, no. 34, Nov. 1983.

Lake Placid Conferences on Home Economics. Proceedings of the First to Tenth Conferences 1899–1908. Lake Placid, New York: 1902.

Lawrence, Judith K., and Kenneth C. Green. *A Question of Quality: The Higher Education Ratings Game.* AAHE-ERIC/Higher Education Research Report, no. 5, Washington, D.C.: American Association for Higher Education, 1980.

Lerner, Gerda. *The Majority Finds Its Past: Placing Women in History.* New York: Oxford Press, 1979.

_____. "The Rise of Feminist Consciousness." In *All of Us Are Present: The Stephens College Symposium. Women's Education: The Future,* Eleanor M. Bender, Bobbie Burk, and Nancy Walker, eds. Columbia: James Madison Wood Research Institute, 1984.

Margulies, Rebecca Zames, and Peter Blau. "The Pecking Order of the Elite: America's Leading Professional Schools." *Change* (November 1973): 21–32.

McLachlan, Mildred Howitson. "The Role of the Home Economics Profession in the Reproduction of Social Relations: An Exploration of Selected Theoretical and Historical Questions." Ph.D. diss., Michigan State University, 1982.

Mitchell, Lucy Sprague. *Pioneering in Education.* Oral history interview conducted by Irene M. Prescott. Regional Oral History Office, Bancroft

Library, University of California, Berkeley, 1962.

_____. *Two Lives: The Story of Wesley Clair Mitchell and Myself*. New York: Simon and Schuster, 1953.

Morgan, Agnes Fay. "Closing Remarks." Reprinted from a symposium honoring Dr. Agnes Fay Morgan's fiftieth anniversary at the University of California, Berkeley, in the *Journal of Nutrition*, supp. 1, part 2 of vol. 91 (February 1967): 65–67.

_____. "High School Courses in Science of the Household, Nutrition, and Citizen-Homemaking." *The School Review* 1, no. 24 (May 1927): 518–29.

_____ "The History of Nutrition and Home Economics in the University of California, Berkeley, 1914–1962." University of California Archives, Bancroft Library, Berkeley, 1962.

_____. "Home Economics Courses and the Higher Institutions of Learning." *The School Review* 28, no. 7 (September 1920): 534–47.

_____. Oral history interview conducted by Alexander Callow. *Centennial History Project*. Regional Oral History Office, Bancroft Library, University of California, Berkeley, 1959.

_____. "Let's Consider Home Economics." *Omicron Nu* 3, no. 40 (winter 1947): 3–6.

_____. "A New Look for the Old-Fashioned Liberal Education of Women." *American Association of University Professors Bulletin* 39, no. 2 (summer 1953).

_____. "Professional Training the Major Concern." *The Journal of Home Economics* 43, no. 4 (April 1951): 253–56.

_____, ed. *A History of Iota Sigma Pi*. University of California Archives, Brancroft Library, University of California, Berkeley, 1963.

Nerad, Maresi. *Doctoral Education at the University of California and Factors Affecting Time to Degree*. Oakland: Office of the President, University of California, 1991.

_____. "Gender Stratification in Higher Education: The Department of Home Economics at the University of California, Berkeley 1916–1962." *Women's Studies International Forum* 10, no. 2 (1987): 157–64.

_____. rev. *In the Company of Educated Women*, by Barbara Miller Solomon, *Women's Studies International Forum* 10, no. 4, (1987): 471–72.

_____. "The Situation of Women at Berkeley between 1870 and 1915." *Feminist Issues* 7, no. 1 (Spring 1987): 67–80.

Newcomer, Mabel. *A Century of Higher Education for American Women*. New York: Harper and Brothers, 1959.

Newman, Louise M., ed. *Men's Ideas / Women's Realities*. New York: Pergamon Press, 1985.

Nutrition Research 22, no. 1 (October 1968).

Oakland Tribune, 1922–1931.

Okey, Ruth, Barbara Kennedy Johnson, Gordon Mackinney. "Agnes Fay

Morgan, 1884–1968." In *In Memoriam*. Berkeley, University of California, May 1969.

_____. "Agnes Fay Morgan (1884–1968)—A Biographical Sketch." *The Journal of Nutrition* 104, no. 9 (September 1974): 1103–07.

_____. "Experiences of a Woman Trained in Science in the Years Preceding the Formation of the Present Department of Nutritional Sciences at UC Berkeley." Nutritional Sciences Library, University of California, Berkeley, 1981.

Olin, Helen R. *The Women of a State University*. New York: G. P. Putnam's Sons, The Knickerbocker Press, 1909.

Olney, Mary McLean. *Oakland, Berkeley, and the University of California*. Oral history interviewed by Willa Baum. Regional Oral History Office, Bancroft Library, University of California, Berkeley, 1963.

Otten, Michael. *University Authority and the Student*. Berkeley: University of California Press, 1970.

Porch, Louise W. "Home Economics: Trends and Developments, 1909–52." Ph.D. diss., Stanford University, 1955.

Powers, Jane Bernard. *The "Girl Question" in Education: Vocation Education for Young Women in the Progressive Era*. London: The Falmer Press, 1992.

The Prytaneans: An Oral History, 1901–1920. vol. 1. Regional Oral History Project. Bancroft Library, University of California, Berkeley, 1970.

Raacke, I. D. "Agnes Fay Morgan." In *Notable American Women: The Modern Period*, Barbara Sicherman, Carol Hurd Green with Ilene Kantrov, Harriette Walker, eds. Cambridge: The Belknap Press of Harvard, 1980.

The Record, 1905.

The Regents' Minutes, 1905–1960.

Register: Officers and Students,1915/1916, University of California Archives, Bancroft Library, Berkeley.

Report of the President of the University, 1890–1920. University of California Archives, Bancroft Library, Berkeley.

A Restudy of the Needs of California in Higher Education. Sacramento: California State Department of Education, 1955.

Ritter, Mary Bennett. *More Than Gold in California*. Berkeley: University of California Press, 1933.

Rosaldo, Michelle Zimbalist, and Loise Lamphere, eds. *Women, Culture and Society*. Stanford: Stanford University Press, 1974.

Rosenberg, Rosalind. *Beyond Separate Spheres*. New Haven: Yale University Press, 1982.

Rossiter, Margaret. *Women Scientists in America: Before Affirmative Action, 1940–1972*. Baltimore: The Johns Hopkins University Press, 1995.

_____. *Women Scientists in America: Struggles and Strategies to 1940*. Baltimore: The Johns Hopkins University Press, 1982.

Rothman, Sheila. *Women's Proper Place: A History of Changing Ideals and Practices, 1870 to the Present*. New York: Basic Books, 1978.

Rudolph, Frederick. *The American College and University: A History*. New York: Alfred Knopf, 1962.

_____. *Curriculum*. San Francisco: Jossey-Bass Publishers, 1977.

Ryerson, Knowles. *The World Is My Campus*. Oral history interviews conducted by Joann Larkey. Shields Library, University of California, Davis, 1977.

San Francisco Chronicle, 1912–1930.

Shapiro, Laura. *Perfection Salad*. New York: Farrar, Straus, and Giroux, 1986.

Simon, Herbert A. *Administrative Behavior*. 3d ed. New York: The Free Press, 1976.

Sokoloff, Natalie. *Between Money and Love: The Dialectics of Women's Home and Market Work*. New York: Praeger, 1981.

Solomon, Barbara Miller. *In the Company of Educated Women*. New Haven: Yale University Press, 1985.

Southmayd, Edna. "Careers in Nutrition." *Nutrition Research* 22, no. 1 (October 1968): 1–4.

Spender, Dale. *Women of Ideas and What Men Have Done to Them: From Aphra Behn to Adrienne Rich*. London: Routledge and Kegan Paul, 1982.

Stadtman, Verne A. *The University of California, 1868–1968: A Centennial Publication of the University of California*. San Francisco: McGraw-Hill, 1970.

Stage, Sara, and Virginia Vincenti. *Rethinking Home Economics*. Ithaca, N.Y.: Cornell University Press, 1997.

Student Opinion, 1915.

Summer Session University of California Bulletin, 1900–1920.

Talbot, Marion, and Lois Kimball Mathews Rosenberry. *The History of the American Association of University Women, 1881–1931*. Boston: The Riverside Press, Cambridge, 1931.

Trow, Martin. "Higher Education as Stratification System: The Analysis of Status." In *Perspectives on Higher Education: Eight Disciplinary and Comparative Views*, Burton Clark, ed. Berkeley: University of California Press, 1984.

The University Chronicle, 1900–1920.

University Course Catalogue, 1900–1962.

Van Hise, Charles. "Education Tendencies in State Universities." *Educational Review* 34, 1907: 504–20.

Veysey, Laurence R. *The Emergence of the American University*. Chicago: The University of Chicago Press, 1965.

Vincenti, Virginia Bramble. "A History of the Philosophy of Home Economics." Ph.D. diss., Pennsylvania State University, 1981.

Webster, David. "America's Highest Ranked Graduate Schools, 1925–1982." *Change* (May/June 1983): 14–24.

Wechsler, Harold S. "An Academic Gresham's Law: Group Repulsion as a Theme in American Higher Education." *Teachers College Record* 82, no. 4 (Summer 1981): 567–88.

Wellman, Harry. *Teaching, Research, and Administration, University of California 1925–1968*. Oral history interview conducted by Malca Challin. Regional Oral History Office, Bancroft Library, University of California, Berkeley, 1976.

Welter, Barbara. "The Cult of True Womenhood: 1820–1860." In *Women's Experience in America*, Esther Katz and Anita Rapone, eds. New Brunswick, N.J.: Transaction Books, 1980.

Willard, Emma. *An Address to the Public*. Published by Middlebury College on the 100th anniversary of the issue of the first edition. Middlebury: Vermont, 1918.

Williamson, Maude. "The Evolution of Homemaking Education." Ph.D. diss., Stanford University, 1942.

The Women's Faculty Club of the University of California, Berkeley, 1919–1982. Oral History Series Conducted 1981–82. Regional Oral History Office, Bancroft Library, University of California, Berkeley, 1983.

Woody, Thomas. *A History of Women's Education in the United States*. 2 vols. New York: Science Press, 1929.

INDEX

187

193

The Challenge of Eastern Asian Education: Implications for America—
William K. Cummings and Philip G. Altbach (eds.)

*Conversations with Educational Leaders: Contemporary Viewpoints on
Education in America*—Anne Turnbaugh Lockwood

*Managed Professionals: Unionized Faculty and Restructuring Academic
Labor*—Gary Rhoades

The Curriculum: Problems, Politics, and Possibilities, Second Edition—
Landon E. Beyer and Michael W. Apple (eds.)

*Education / Technology / Power: Educational Computing as a Social
Practice*—Hank Bromley and Michael W. Apple (eds.)

Capitalizing Knowledge: New Intersections of Industry and Academia—
Henry Etzkowitz, Andrew Webster, and Pat Healey (eds.)

*The Academic Kitchen: A Social History of Gender Stratification at the
University of California, Berkeley*—Maresi Nerad